Christian
Community:
Response
to Reality

Christian Community: Response to Reality

BERNARD J. COOKE

Holt, Rinehart and Winston
NEW YORK • CHICAGO • SAN FRANCISCO • ATLANTA
DALLAS • MONTREAL • TORONTO • LONDON • SYDNEY

Copyright © 1970 by Holt, Rinehart and Winston, Inc.
All rights reserved
Library of Congress Catalog Card Number: 77-102022
SBN: 03-084306-9 College   SBN: 03-084-557-2 Trade
Quotations from the Old and New Testaments are taken from the
Catholic edition of the Revised Standard Version of the Bible
Printed in the United States of America

Contents

PREFACE   vii

1   Authority for Freedom's Sake   1
Freedom and Authority, 2;
The Authority of Knowledge, 4;
The Authority of Love, 9;
Authority and Community, 13;
An Authority of Service, 18;
The Authority of Peter, 22;
Ministries in the Church, 24;
Authority and Obedience, 27

2   Mission to the World   31
The World and the Kingdom, 34;
The Hour of the Lord, 37;
The Messianic Mission, 40;
Church and Evangelization, 45;
The Mission of the Christian Community, 49;
The Role of the Institution, 58

3   The Changing Church   62
Change and Tradition, 63;
Change and the Scriptures, 65;
Change and the Christian Community, 68;
Lessons from History, 70; Creed, 75;
Cult, 82; Community, 88

4 Word of God or Words of Men 95
The Limitations of Language, 96;
The Word of Yahweh, 99; The Word of Jesus, 108;
The Word of God Today, 116;
The Christian Conscience, 120;
Scripture, Sacrament, Tradition, 121

5 The Worship of Life 127
Worship in the Old Testament, 129;
Jesus and Worship, 130; Life as Worship, 134;
Worship and Social Justice, 135;
Worship as Symbol, 140; Christian Sacraments, 145;
Baptism, Transfiguration, The Last Supper, 147;
Sacramental Worship, 155

6 God, Hidden and Revealed 158
The Challenge of Secularity, 158;
Myths and the Divine, 160;
Philosophy and the Divine, 162;
The Faith of Israel, 165; Jesus and the Divine, 169;
The Faith of Christians, 177;
The Role of the Spirit, 183;
The Church: Sacrament of Christ, 185

Preface

THIS VOLUME is meant to complement an earlier companion work, THE GOD OF SPACE AND TIME, and to pursue that volume's objective of applying the insights of the Scriptures to the key religious questions of men today.

In our world, which has been called "a world come of age," there is increased questioning of the need for and value of the Church. Theological attention is no longer concentrated on deciding which Christian Church is to be preferred to others. Even the ecumenical discussions about the ways of reuniting the divided Christian community seem to be losing some impetus. A more radical question has come to the fore: Is there any purpose for an organized Christian religious body? What is termed "Christian secularity" — involvement in a serious and dedicated attempt to better human life — is being suggested as a response to the Gospel that is more authentic and ultimate than participation in organized Church life and ritualized worship.

These "attacks" on the familiar patterns and structures of life in the Christian Church cannot be dismissed lightly. Certainly, much about the Church needs positive criticism and reform; and if reform is to reach beyond token adjustments to modern life and bring about a true revitalization of Christianity, Christians cannot avoid posing the most telling and basic questions about the Church.

Has not mankind passed culturally beyond a real need for organized religion? Specifically, does the institutionally organized Church make sense as a contemporary expression of God's saving action in the world? Is not an authoritatively governed religious community out of date in our day, when the freedom and personal autonomy of each man and woman is being increasingly appreciated?

But the questions go even deeper. Does religion, in any form, make sense? Is it really possible for men to "contact" God, and to deal personally with the divine? Was not such religious activity a "myth" that men needed in past generations, in order to make their life meaningful and bearable? Perhaps contemporary man, armed with scientific understanding of himself and his world and with the technology required to transform his world, can dispense with this "myth of God" and more intelligently accept the secularity of his human existence.

While the Old and New Testament writings cannot be expected to give specific answers to these modern questions, they may provide the insights that can guide us today as we confront the religious questions of our world. Obviously, the Scriptures will speak in this fashion only to men and women of faith. It is to such believers that the following chapters are directed. Hopefully, these pages will manifest somewhat the enduring relevance of the Bible and lead to intensified reading of the Bible itself.

BERNARD J. COOKE

CHAPTER ONE

Authority
for Freedom's Sake

IF THERE IS one thing that is clear in the Bible it is the teaching that God desires freedom for men. The divine action as it is described in Old Testament times is one of liberation. This action finds its highest expression in Christ, who has come so that men might be free. This freedom is intended for all men, without distinction, whether they are rich or poor, educated or unschooled, Jew or Gentile, male or female.

This is the unmistakable message of the Gospel of Jesus Christ, the Gospel that the Church has been preaching to men for two millenia. It is paradoxical that the Church is for many people today a symbol for the denial of freedom, an authority-figure that stands in opposition to man's efforts at achieving a truly mature self-determination. To the extent that this is the case, the Church is not fulfilling her function, which is to sacramentalize the freeing activity of the risen Christ, but is a "scandal" in the strictest sense of that term — a countersign that prevents men from hearing the Gospel of Christ.

This charge has probably been leveled against Roman Catholics more than any other group of Christians, because authority-figures (like the pope) are so prominent in the Roman Catholic Church, and their exercise of power so well-publicized. Unfortunately, a fair share of the criticism is justified by the history of the past few centuries. During this time the authority in the Roman Catholic Church (as well as in many other Christian Churches) has found itself on more than one occasion allied with oppressive governments and with the affluent and powerful elements of society.

Today most Christians would like to feel that this anti-freedom stand of the Church is past history, and that now the situation has been reversed. Certainly, a drastic change of attitude has taken place within the past century (providentially aided by historical factors, such as the abolition of the papal states in the late nineteenth century), but it would be naive to think that the problem is completely solved. The well-established "authority crisis" within the Roman Catholic Church is a clear indication that the problem still awaits solution, even though one may be coming rapidly.

In the movement towards a solution, which will inevitably be painful for many people, it is critically important that the special nature of authority and obedience as they apply to the Church's life be recognized. It would be a serious error, and the cause of no end of useless controversy and suffering, to argue for or against some false understanding of authority. Christians today are faced with a very serious question: Is Christianity compatible with the thrust of men towards freedom and dignity and equality, or is it an outdated social structure that stands in the way of genuine human development? In dealing with this question they must not be hampered by a faulty knowledge of what authority is truly meant to be in the Church's life. An immature acceptance of illegitimate claims to authority would make no more sense than an unthinking rejection of all authority in Christian faith and community existence.

Freedom and Authority

What we can learn from a careful study of God's liberating activity in human history, as this is revealed to us in sacred Scripture, is that authority and freedom must coexist. Freedom can only be preserved and developed in a social context which is stable and ordered because a legitimate authority guides a society in law and justice. The origin and evolution of Old Testament Israel is a classic example of this principle. From the very beginning of Israel's history, in the exodus from Egypt and entry into the promised land, Yahweh's action is one of freeing his people. At the same time it is an action of uniting them into a people through a covenant, which is grounded in the Israelites' acceptance of the law that Yahweh gives them (Ex. 24). Both liberation and covenant law come through the mediation of Moses, who remains throughout Old Testament tradition a major and controlling authority-figure.

The inner relation of law to freedom is illustrated by Israel's law, which in its written and codified form or in its oral promulgation by lawgivers, was a necessary condition for the continuing existence of the people. Without this law to guide their social development, they would either have lapsed into chaos or been absorbed into the cultures that surrounded them. The law was a key influence in establishing and preserving their national identity. The law was meant to protect the poor and weak from oppression; it guaranteed the fundamental dignity of each Israelite as a member of the covenant.

Whatever may have been the actual historical role of Moses in the origins of the chosen people, the traditions attribute to him an authority which continues throughout Israel's history. The very glorification of Moses as lawgiver and leader in the sacred writings and oral traditions that were passed on from generation to generation helps establish a pattern of authoritative direction of the people. Such authority was provided, though in sporadic and informal fashion, by the judges, those charismatic leaders who helped preserve Israel as a people during the first two or three centuries after the entry into the promised land. From 1000 B.C. onward, the authoritative structures of the kingship provided a more clearly organized and permanent direction for Israel. And even though the kingship did not fare too well in the historical evolution of the people, the role of the king was taken over in large measure during the post-exilic period by the Jerusalem Temple priesthood, particularly by the high priest.

There is nothing unique about the fact that Israel as an enduring social reality was governed by men who claimed and exercised authority. Societies seem naturally to demand such authority. Nor is it peculiar to Israel to have those in authority claiming divine origin for their official power; history knows innumerable variants of a "divine right of kings" justification for governmental authority. What is characteristic of Israel, in theory if not always in practice, is the insistence that all authority in Israel is really Yahweh's: He alone is ultimately the king; all other rulers only represent him and act by way of delegation. One of the clearest reflections of this attitude is the Israelitic view of law. All law is seen as coming from Yahweh. He may use human mediators to communicate the law, Moses especially, but it is he whose will and direction is expressed in the law. And Israel never did produce any royal or strictly civil law.

With Christianity the immanence of divine authority in the life of the religious community is stressed even more. All authority that is operative in the Church is that of the risen Christ; he alone is the Lord. What the New Testament literature points out, however, is that Christ's authority is quite different than men might expect; it is exercised in a manner that not only permits but demands a mature, free response from his followers.

Once the nature of Christ's authority and the manner of its continued exercise in the life of the Church is understood, there is no theoretical possibility of opposition between authority and freedom in Christianity. The difficulty is rather in the practical order. Much of this difficulty can be traced simply to the fact that it is human beings who exercise positions of authority in the Church, and they can abuse these positions. Much of the problem has also been caused historically by a less than adequate understanding of the kind of authority that should function in the life of the Christian community.

The Authority of Knowledge

One thing to be kept in mind in examining the authority of the Church is that "authority" is not a univocal notion. There are many kinds of authority, distinct in form and origin. Two types require special examination because they are related to the authority that is proper to Christianity: the authority possessed by one who *knows,* one who is an expert in a particular field of human understanding and whom we therefore call "an authority" on this or that subject; and the authority possessed by one who *loves* another, the authority of a friend.

Men have always recognized that possession of knowledge is a source of authority. The statement, "knowledge is power," is not a new one. One sees this statement in advertising posters today that urge young people, particularly of minority groups, to continue with their education. But every oppressed or minority group in history has known that it had to obtain education for its children; they had to move into the world of knowledge, if they hoped to gain equality and dignity in society.

Today the power of knowledge is recognized as perhaps never before. Because of the increasing complexity of our technology and the urbanization that has accompanied it, we are ever more dependent upon scientific research, creative social thinking, and technical knowledge in a wide variety of fields. The future belongs to those peoples who can produce the best thinkers. Minds are recognized today as a country's most important natural resource, and many countries of the world (where life is less affluent or scientific study less advanced) are deeply concerned about the "brain drain" — the emigration of their best minds to countries which seem to offer greater opportunity.

Our purpose here, however, is not to reflect upon these important social problems but to show how the present situation makes clear that intrinsic authority comes with knowledge. The well-educated person, has both the ability (a certain kind of power) and the right to speak authoritatively about those things he really knows. This is not a question of a snobbishness that can come from such things as a college degree; it is something much more basic. Either one knows something or he does not. If he does know, he has the ability, the right, and the responsibility to communicate this knowledge. Such is the authority proper to the teacher.

The teacher who effectively and honestly exercises this authority does so in order to lead others to freedom. The teacher who attempts to keep others in dependence upon himself and his own insights, who does not work to make his students increasingly autonomous through their own understanding, has failed. A teacher's purpose is to extend men's knowledge. As this knowledge is extended, the range of choices open to men in their decision-making is broadened, and the decisions made are now dependent upon others' understanding of them rather than on faith in those who made the decisions.

Nothing is so enslaving, so inimical to free choice, as the denial to people of the knowledge that is their right. Without knowledge, men cannot even know the possible choices that exist. Historically, one of the standard means of keeping a populace in subjection was to keep it in ignorance, to control the channels of news and information, to "brainwash" persons by denying to them any contact with knowledge that might lead to decisions which would threaten the power of the ruling group. Removal of such ignorance is an essential step in liberating people; to do this is the function of a teacher. In communicating knowledge to men and women, the teacher opens up to them the various possibilities of human life and activity. He becomes an important agent in making them free.

What is true of the human teacher is eminently true of God in that act of teaching which we call "revelation." This revelation is meant to open up to men a whole new horizon of understanding — vistas and insights that men could never have attained if they had been left to their own powers of knowledge. In the light of this new understanding of reality, which Scripture tells us is a communication of God's own wisdom, men can come to a wise determination of their own lives and destinies — and this is the heart of true freedom.

Reading the Old Testament literature, we become aware that the process of divine direction that characterized the historical experience of the Israelites was one of leading this people away from the errors which would have enslaved them. The understanding of human life that came to the Israelites in this way, the understanding of the world in which man lives, of the forces that work in his world, and of Yahweh's providential care of his people, did much to free them from the kind of superstitious fears that form a major barrier to the liberty of the human spirit.

Through Moses, the prophets, and the other charismatic leaders of Old Testament times who spoke with the authority of "the word of Yahweh," Israel was gradually led towards the truth and wisdom that make men free. Israel's history was shaped in large measure by her great teachers, men who possessed a unique authority among their contemporaries (even when they were persecuted, as many of the prophets were) because they possessed the special understanding of life that was communicated to them in the process of divine revelation.

Early Christianity, as the prologue of John's Gospel clearly indicates, believed that Jesus of Nazareth possessed in unparalleled fashion this kind of authority. He was "the teacher" par excellence. Even Moses faded into a secondary role. Moses was the mediator of the law, which had indeed provided guidance and unity for Old Testament Israel, but Jesus is the truth itself, the very source of liberation. United to the Father in that incomparable relationship which is proper to him as the Father's own son, Jesus can speak out of his own immediate experience. He is an authority on the topic of divinity as no other man could possibly be, for he is God's own word incarnated.

The Gospels tell us that the crowds who listened to Jesus' teaching during the years of his public ministry sensed his authority as he spoke. "The crowds were astonished at his teaching, for he taught them as one who had authority, and not as their scribes" (Mt. 7:28-29). Apparently, many of Jesus' hearers began to look on him as a prophet. It is clear from the New Testament texts that the early Christians, once Christ's death and resurrection had occurred, saw him as the culmination and fulfillment of the entire Old Testament prophetic movement. The prophets had been Yahweh's messengers, his servants, sent to convert Israel to her covenant pledges. Jesus is God's own son, sent to establish the new covenant through his death and resurrection (Mt. 21:37-42). Other prophets, the last and greatest of whom was John the Baptist, could bear witness to the light; Jesus himself was that light, the light which is the very life of men (Jn. 1:9).

Yet, if Jesus did possess such knowledge, and therefore such unprecedented authority to teach, it was only so that he might thereby lead men to freedom. Luke's Gospel tells us how Jesus, early in his first Galilean ministry, came back to the synagogue of Nazareth. There in the Sabbath service, he laid claim to being a prophet in fulfillment of the passage from Isaiah (1:1-2) that he read to them:

> The Spirit of the Lord God is upon me,
>   because the Lord has anointed me
> to bring good tidings to the afflicted; he has sent
>   me to bind up the brokenhearted,
> to proclaim liberty to the captives, and the opening
>   of the prison to those who are bound. . . .

It is impossible to miss the emphasis on liberation, on freedom from oppression, that marks this Isaian passage that found fulfillment in Jesus' life and teaching.

One of the most striking passages in New Testament writing is the eleventh chapter of Matthew's Gospel, which bears on the point we are discussing. The chapter is a carefully worked-out claim that Jesus is not only a greater teacher than the rabbis, not only the greatest of the prophets, not only wiser than the scribes — wiser, even, than Solomon himself — but he is wisdom itself. He can demand that men listen to him precisely because he possesses that understanding of reality which alone can free men from evil. "All things have been delivered to me by my Father; and no one knows the Son except the Father, and no one knows the Father except the Son and anyone to whom the Son chooses to reveal him" (Mt. 11:27). And the "proof" to which Jesus points in this scene to justify such a claim to wisdom is his work of liberating the poor and the oppressed: "Go and tell John what you hear and see: the blind receive their sight and the lame walk, lepers are cleansed and the deaf hear, and the dead are raised up, and the poor have good news preached to them" (Mt. 11:4-5).

The view of Jesus' ministry found in the New Testament, is, plainly, that Christ teaches and acts as he does because he has the authority to do so. This authority is the authority of truth itself, and of one who possesses truth. And this authority is used by Jesus with only one purpose: to free men for life. This is the very nature of truth — it is the root of freedom.

The need to free men by the power of truth did not end with the death and resurrection of Christ. In the pentecostal gift of Christ's own Spirit (Acts 2), a gift that continues throughout the Church's historical existence, the Christian community receives a prophetic commission. The Christian people and the Spirit himself in the midst of this people are to proclaim to all men the "good news" of man's liberation from sin and death, the Gospel of Jesus' death and resurrection. This preaching is, like Jesus' preaching, a word spoken with authority, because the Spirit works in and through the words of men. Actually, because the prophetic word of the Christian community expresses the presence of the Spirit whom the risen Christ shares with Christians, the authority that this word carries is the authority of the risen Lord himself. Whatever special authority the Church possesses in her teaching ministry is the authority of Christ who continues to teach mankind in and through this Church.

The Authority of Love

There is a second kind of authority that one person can exercise in relation to another, that of *love*. This is a mysterious and unstructured type of authority, but it is real and important in our human experience. If one loves another and the love is accepted, it gives the one who loves a certain power over his friend, a certain right to direct the other's life and decisions. This is not the right and power to dictate, or to exploit, or to dominate; all of these are false and selfish and weak misunderstandings of what love truly is. But if someone is truly my friend, I have a right by virtue of our friendship (and also an obligation) to urge him to grow and develop as a person, to become the person I would like to see him become, to achieve the good of which I think him capable. Such authority is meant to function in many human relationships: between parents and children, husband and wife, teachers and students, friends with one another. And if the authority is exercised carefully and honestly, as a genuine expression of one's loving concern for another, it is a creative influence, life-giving and liberating.

Faith, as it is expressed in both the Old and New Testaments, tells us that God's authority over men is this kind of authority in love. It is true that God has authority over men because he is the creator and therefore the Lord of life. But God creates man and keeps him in existence because he loves man; his directives to men (his laws) are given so that men will achieve the joy and greatness that a loving God desires for them.

Long before Jesus of Nazareth spoke in this manner about his Father "who so loved the world," the prophets and other great teachers of Old Testament Israel began to realize the incredible fact of Yahweh's love for his people. Yahweh was the Lord, and he did insist on the observance of his covenant law. But the very reality of his speaking to Israel and expressing his will in the law was an act of revelation, an act of personal communication, an act of self-giving — and self-giving is the essence of personal love.

We must not suppose that the Israelites immediately grasped the profoundly personal nature of Yahweh's dealings with them. They did not. In the early centuries of the people's existence, "when Israel was a child," the prevailing attitude toward Yahweh was probably one of awe and fear, a willingness to follow his laws in order to gain his protection and avoid his punishment. By the time of the great charismatic prophets, the imagery used in the biblical literature indicates that the religious insight of Israel has grown, that the personal aspect of Yahweh's dealings is slowly being appreciated.

Hosea speaks of Yahweh as the husband of Israel, a god who punishes the infidelity of his people but who does so in order to win back the people's devotion (Hos. 2). Isaiah describes Yahweh as the owner of a vineyard (Israel) who devotedly takes care of the vines he has selected and planted in a choice spot (Is. 5). Yahweh is a god to be feared by those who desert him and do evil, but he is the support of the oppressed, their rock and their stronghold (Is. 25:4; 26:4). Jeremiah uses the imagery of his prophetic predecessors, but adds to it the picture of Yahweh as a shepherd gathering together the sheep which had been dispersed (the Israelites in exile), an image that is then used to great effect by Ezekiel during the Babylonian exile (Jer. 23:3; Ezek. 34).

Perhaps the most constant indication in the prophetic literature of this more personal view of Yahweh is the fact that the prophets, when they foretell the punishment that is to come to the people for their sinfulness, do not speak of Yahweh as a tyrant who ruthlessly crushes those who break his laws, but as a lover who has been betrayed, as a father whose children have ungratefully rebelled against him. The prophets, evidently, already had some insight into the fact that the deepest level of Yahweh's authority over his people lay not in his power to reward or punish, but in his love for them.

Jesus' prophetic message leaves no doubt: his Father, whom the Jews had worshipped under the name of "Yahweh," loves men with a love that baffles human understanding. Not because men deserve it, but simply out of his love, this Father has sent his own Son, his own Word, to speak for him in human form. The concern and love of Jesus for men is itself the sign, the sacrament, of his Father's love and of the kind of authority that his Father employs to establish his kingdom in the hearts of men.

In Jesus' own ministry, as he exercised it during his

earthly career and as he continues to exercise it as the risen Lord, it is his love that gives him authority in men's lives. His love, like all personal love, is demanding. It demands a response in love; it has a right to claim that response. In the Gospel accounts what Jesus asked is unmistakable. He wanted the person: "Go, sell what you have and give it to the poor; and come *follow me.*" This is a new, simple, but all-embracing law; it encompasses the totality of a person's life and activity.

Our own experience of human love teaches us that love is profoundly liberating. Love lays on us responsibilities of the most demanding sort; it requires us to share the thing to which we cling most tightly, our own self; it brings with it risks that are more frightening than any others in our lives. But it is love that frees a person to be truly honest and genuinely himself; it vitalizes his experience so that he lives fully; it stimulates and brightens his consciousness and his thought. Truth will make a man free, but a man must love truth before he seeks it. Knowledge is liberating, but the most important kind of knowledge is knowing other persons, and one cannot truly know another person unless he loves him.

This is why Christ, when he is exercizing his authority as the supreme lawgiver of human history, can give one simple law: "A new commandment I give to you, that you love one another" (Jn. 13:34). And this is how Christ will establish his kingdom, which is also the kingdom of his Father. A king is one who rules; he will be truly a king in proportion as he rules not just the external behavior of men (which any tyrant can do through physical coercion), but their inner life. There is only one way to guide and direct the inner consciousness and motivations of men: get them to love what you wish them to love. Christ has done this by giving himself to men in his death and resurrection, so that this self-gift will win men's love in return. " 'I, when I am lifted up from the earth, will draw all men to myself.' He said this to show by what death he was to die" (Jn. 12:32-33).

There is no doubt, then, from the New Testament writings,

that Christ's authority is the kind that flows from knowledge and love. Since the Church possesses no other legitimate authority than that of Christ, in which she shares, the authority proper to the life of the Christian community — both within the community itself and in its redemptive activity in the world — must be of this same kind.

That Christ exercises his authority by teaching and loving is one of several indications in revelation that God's redemptive action leads men towards being more truly human. Men will be human to the degree they are free; to be free they must know and love; to know and love they must be taught and loved — and this is what Christ does in and through his body which is the Church. To those who are his followers in the Church, he communicates an understanding of his Gospel, and does this through the very structures of that community. To those who are the members of the Church, through their love and concern for one another, he gives his own love. In this way he works to free them, so that they in turn can free their fellow men.

Authority and Community

Genuine human freedom, as it is envisaged by the biblical literature, can come into being only if men form a true community. From our ordinary experience we know that the processes of communication we call "teaching" and "learning" require some stable grouping of people to be consistent and profitable. Personal communication is built upon and builds community. Experience also shows that love among men can come into being and develop only if people have the opportunity to deal with one another, share experiences together, develop common concerns — in short, to live together in some form of community.

God's action in both Old Testament Israel and Christianity has been one of forming such a community, so that true freedom might be achieved. Our religious thinking has for several centuries been so individualistic that it is difficult for us to grasp and appreciate the *corporate* reality of salvation as the

Israelites and the early Christians experienced it. In recent years, we have slowly been regaining some understanding of this communal aspect of salvation and religion. This has happened because of biblical studies which drew our attention to the manner of God's dealings with the people whose experience is recorded in the Bible.

We cannot establish with certainty what historical happenings actually initiated the Old Testament dispensation. But connected with the traditions of exodus and covenant and entry into the land there is one undeniable historical fact: the beginnings of what we think of as Old Testament faith and religion are identical with the emergence of this people Israel. Not only does God give the Old Testament stage of his revelation to this believing people; this people Israel, evolving as a community of faith, *is* God's Old Testament revelation. This people is what gives expression to God's special saving presence.

Certainly, there were charismatic individuals who provided leadership for this communal experience, men whom the traditions of Israel describe as specially endowed with Yahweh's spirit. Upon such men and their special awareness of Yahweh's presence and "word" the religious advance of Israel was largely dependent. Yet these men — and the great charismatic prophets come immediately to mind, though they are not the only examples — were specially gifted by Yahweh *for the sake of the whole people*. They were sent to the people; they functioned within the traditions and experience of the people, and actually drew more deeply from these sources than did their contemporaries. Their role in Israel's life was to make the people precisely that: a people, a community grounded in Yahweh's covenant with them.

So prominent is the corporate nature of Israel's early faith-experience and religious expression that the individual seems obscured and de-emphasized. Part of the evolution of Old Testament thought is the gradually growing awareness of the individual Israelite's responsibility, merit, and culpability (this is another facet of the emerging consciousness of individual freedom and its importance). By the time of Jeremiah one can find explicit texts that say: Each man bears the burden of his own choice, the burden of his own sin, or the glory of his own good deeds. However, this deepening discovery of the autonomy and importance of the individual does not detract from the essentially social character of the Israelites' relationship to Yahweh.

The social reality of Israel — a community based on faith and covenant — is meant to guarantee protection and support for the weaker elements of society, the poor and the orphan and the widow. The law of Israel, in those provisions which govern the various conflict-areas of the people's daily life, is meant to safeguard the interests of the weak. It is the weak and oppressed of any society who need the law for protection; the powerful will always manage to further their own interests. In their call to Israel to return to the observance of Yahweh's law and to fidelity to his covenant, the prophets are unanimous in insisting on the fundamental importance of social justice.

Yahweh's purpose was to form for himself a people which would dwell in peace and joy on the land he gave it. Yet, the prophets say, this purpose is being defeated by the avarice and venality of the very ones, the leaders of the people, who should be using their authority to preserve justice and freedom. Abuse of authority by king and priests and official prophets has intensified the division between rich and poor; Israel no longer exists as a true community of faith.

Jesus took up this prophetic message and charged the leadership of his day with the same kind of misuse of law. "Woe to you, scribes and Pharisees, hypocrites! for you tithe mint and dill and cummin, and have neglected the weightier matters of the law, justice and mercy and faith" (Mt. 23:23). Like the Old Testament prophets, he challenged men to make personal decisions. He demanded a response from those to whom he preached the kingdom of his Father. It is difficult to see how the person's freedom and choice and conscience could be more clearly emphasized than it is in the New Testament writings.

The New Testament literature also speaks about the corporate unity of the Church as something that far outstrips the unity possessed by Israel. The Christian community is the body of Christ, with the kind of unity proper to a living organism. In that body each member has a function to play, just as in the human body (Eph. 4:1-16). There is to be no division between rich and poor, between strong and weak. There is to be a basic equality, a basic reverence for one another as persons and fellow Christians; Christ has come to break down all walls of division among men (Eph. 2:11-20). In the Church, therefore, there is to be a unique regard for the inviolability of the individual person, and for exactly this reason the corporate aspect of the Church's life will be more intense and rich. In such a context, men can live with that freedom which is proper to the sons of God.

Neither Jesus nor his first followers were impractical idealists who thought that such freedom would be achieved without effort or suffering, without some structured community life in which tensions would inevitably arise. Paul's first letter to the Corinthian Christians is a marvelous example of this realism. He speaks strongly and clearly about the unity of Christians as the body of Christ, and he is almost harshly outspoken in his denunciation of those who would destroy this unity, particularly by allowing class distinctions to spoil the Eucharist as a true expression of Christian community (1 Cor. 11:17-34).

At the same time, he recognizes the need for distinction of functions in the Corinthian Church. He even seems to accept as inevitable a certain tension between the charismatic and institutional manifestations of the one Spirit of Christ. But in the thirteenth chapter of the letter — which is a classic passage on Christian love — he sees the tensions of community as soluble and even creative if men will truly love one another.

Freedom for men, within the Church and outside it, was the goal of Christ's ministry and the purpose of his death and resurrection. Achievement of this freedom was, and remains, the goal of the Church's existence. Paradoxically, or so it seems at first glance, this demands authority and law in human society as a whole and within the Christian community itself. Law and authority are needed to bind any community of men into an enduring society that can guarantee the context needed for the fostering of true freedom. The key to a secure freedom is the maintenance of justice and true order in a society.

This is not to deny that truth is the foundation of freedom. There can be no denying the biblical statement: "The truth will make you free." But this truth must be translated into the practical, contingent judgments with which both individual men and societies are constantly faced. Some kind of unifying direction, some form of effective leadership, is needed if such pragmatic judgments are to govern a group of human beings.

Such is the ideal of kingship that is sketched in the pages of the Old Testament. When Israel found this ideal so seldom realized in her rulers, she increasingly projected its fulfillment in the figure of the expected Messiah. As the eleventh chapter of Isaiah predicts, the Messiah, when he comes, will be filled with the spirit of the Lord, a spirit of wisdom and understanding and counsel, so that he will be able to judge with truth and equity. An earlier passage in Isaiah tells us that the Messiah will be called "Prince of peace," which is saying practically the same thing, for peace is the situation of true stability that results from the establishment of justice in a society.

Even in the Christian community itself — which, at least ideally, would be a group of men and women bound together in a unity of love grounded in faith in Christ — there is need for some kind of authority. Some guidance and leadership is necessary so that the unity of faith will be preserved. Though the Spirit of Christ is the ultimate guide in this respect, there can be various claimants to the Spirit who, at times, may seriously disagree with one another as to the meaning of the Gospel. Moreover, there is need for some organizing force as Christians undertake the increasingly complex task of transforming human society according to the vision of Christ. Here, again, it is the Spirit who is the moving force behind the mission of the Church, but some human direction is required to translate the inspirations of the Spirit into concrete prudential decisions.

For the moment, we are not describing the need or function of any given authoritative group within the Christian community. Rather, we are pointing to an intrinsic need that apparently exists in any permanent and effective human society. What manner of authority should be exercised in the Church will have to be determined by a careful examination of the New Testament's teaching on the authority of Christ himself. Ultimately, there is no authority that operates in the Church — at least no authentic authority — except that of the risen Christ; he alone is the Lord. Anyone else can legitimately lay claim to authority only in dependence upon Christ.

We have already seen the authority that Jesus claimed and exercised as a prophetic figure, as a teacher of truth and wisdom. This authority flowed from his unique understanding of the Father, from the fact that he was himself the Father's Word. It was, for this reason, an authority far surpassing that of the scribes of his day, of the prophets, and even of Moses himself.

An Authority of Service

But Jesus was the Messiah. The early kerygma and all of the Gospels proclaim his right to this title and his exercise of this office. He not only preaches the kingdom, he is the king. However, his kingdom "is not of this world," his rule over men is unique and unexpected — he rules by serving others.

Paul proclaims this strange claim to "power" in his letter to the Philippians. In the second chapter of the epistle there is a famous passage which some biblical scholars think is a quotation from a liturgical hymn already in common usage in the infant Church. He is urging the Christians of Philippi to "put on the mind of Christ," and he goes on to point out how Jesus, although he already existed as God before the Incarnation and enjoyed the full glory of divinity, did not hesitate to become man and to take on the form of a servant. So thoroughgoing and dedicated was Jesus' service of his fellowmen that he was willing to face even death for them. It was because of this "obedience unto death" that he gained the position of Lord in his resurrection.

We would misread the text from Philippians if we understood it to mean that Jesus' role as Lord replaced his role as servant, as if his service ended with his death and resurrection. Just the opposite is true: It is by his resurrection that Jesus can most fully undertake his mission of serving men, and it is in this service that he functions as Lord. Christ exercises an authority beyond any other figure in human history, yet he does so by submitting himself to the needs of others.

Perhaps by studying a series of New Testament passages we can gain some understanding of this paradoxical kind of authority. In the first of these texts (Mt. 20:25-28), Jesus and the Twelve are depicted on the way to Jerusalem, where Jesus will be put to death. While they walk along, a dispute breaks out among the disciples as they argue over the positions of eminence they hope to occupy in the kingdom that Jesus will establish. Obviously, they are still thinking of an earthly kingdom.

Jesus turns to them and chides them for their lack of understanding, explaining to them the kind of authority that he himself will have and that they will exercise in the early Christian community. He distinguishes his authority from the kind that is appealed to by earthly rulers: The kings of this world rule by domination and by power, but it is not so in his kingdom. Among his followers, the one who wishes to be first must become so by being servant to all the others, "even as the Son of man came not to be served but to serve, and to give his life as a ransom for many."

The full force of this statement hits us when we recognize

it as Jesus' claim to be the fulfillment of the "suffering servant" described in the fourth of the "servant songs" from the
book of Isaiah (52:13 — 53:12). In that Isaian passage the
Servant is one who bears the punishment of his brethren,
though he himself is without guilt; and by his vicarious suffering he wins salvation for others.

> Surely he has borne our griefs
> and carried our sorrows;
> yet we esteemed him stricken,
> smitten by God, and afflicted.
> But he was wounded for our transgressions,
> he was bruised for our iniquities.

What Jesus was doing, then, in the scene described by
Matthew, was pointing out to his disciples the enigmatic nature of authority as it functions in the mystery of Christian
redemption. The political model of authority is radically and
explicitly denied — something that has not always been remembered during the past two thousand years by those in positions of authority in the Church. Instead of acting as temporal rulers do, those who occupy positions of eminence in
the Christian community are to serve their brethren, even to
the point of giving up their life for them.

Essentially the same scene is described by Luke's Gospel in
the second text we wish to examine (Lk. 22:24-30). Luke
has, however, transposed the scene, apparently for theological
reasons, and places the dispute among the disciples at the
Last Supper. At table the Twelve begin arguing about who
will be first. Jesus silences their wrangling by making them
reflect on their situation: He who is unquestionably the Master is acting as their servant during the meal. So, also, in the
kingdom that he is giving to them, they must learn to serve
one another.

This is not an ordinary meal, though. Immediately preceding the verses we have just discussed, Luke's Gospel
gives the account of Jesus' giving himself to his disciples
under the appearances of bread and wine. "And he took
bread, and when he had given thanks he broke it and gave it

to them, saying, 'This is my body which is given for you'."
The "service" he has just performed for his disciples was the
gift of himself to them; the beginning of the Passover act that
is to carry on through death into resurrection. In this death
and resurrection he will give himself irrevocably to them, re-
maining with them "all days, even to the end of the world."

Luke's Gospel, as it describes the Last Supper, shows that
Jesus' own authority and the authority proper to the Church's
life must be understood in the eucharistic context. Immediately after pointing out to his disciples that they are to serve
one another just as he has been serving them, Jesus goes on
to promise them the kingdom: "as my Father appointed a
kingdom for me, so do I appoint for you that you may eat
and drink at my table in my kingdom . . ." (Lk. 22:30).

The action of the Supper, which is carried on through the
Christian celebration of the Eucharist, is the key to authority
in the Church. Authority should be exercised among Christians by the gift of self in love: Christ's self-gift to his followers, Christians' self-gift to one another. Such authority is
meant to be exercised by all who belong to the Church, but it
is expected in special fashion from those who occupy positions of importance in the Church's life.

We find the same teaching in the Pauline tradition, as for
example in Ephesians 5:20-27. The epistle is explaining the
various relationships of authority among Christians —
husbands and wives, parents and children, masters and servants. In describing the relative positions of wife and husband
within the social structure of the family, the epistle tells husbands that they are to exercise their authority as Christ did in
relationship to the Church: "Husbands, love your wives, as
Christ loved the church and gave himself up for her, that he
might sanctify her. . . ."

What we realize in reflecting on this passage, one of the
richest and most profound in Scripture, is the nature of Jesus'
redeeming act. His death and resurrection were an act of
self-surrender, not just to his Father, but to all those who
would be the Church, his bride. As those who are joined in

marriage give up their previous life and independent existence to form a new community, and are so deeply united in the mystery of human love and sexuality that they become "one flesh," so Jesus gave up the earthly life he had known and chose the new life of resurrection, in which he could be united with men in a most profound and redeeming presence. The unity of Christ and Christians that results is so immediate and intimate that the Church becomes truly "the body of Christ."

This, then, was the kind of authority that Jesus claimed and established for himself. During his earthly ministry he had already begun the process of serving men, of providing for their needs and sharing himself and his understanding of truth with them. In his death and resurrection he passes into a new and more complete expression of this same mission. He accomplishes this, above all, by giving his Church his own Spirit of truth and love in the mystery of Pentecost. His risen life is one of continued self-giving to men, so that they may be Christianized. This takes place in special fashion in his eucharistic giving of his body and blood.

This, too, is the basic law that is operative in the life of the Christian community. John's Gospel, again in the context of the Last Supper, states the law simply and unequivocably: "A new commandment I give to you, that you love one another; even as I have loved you, that you also love one another. By this all men will know that you are my disciples, if you have love for one another" (Jn. 13:34-35).

The Authority of Peter

In the light of this New Testament teaching on the nature and origin of Jesus' own human authority, we can understand more fully the texts which the Catholic Church has always used to explain the authority vested in the bishop of Rome, the texts, namely, dealing with Christ's grant of authority to Peter. Our question here is not whether Christ gave authority to Peter, or whether Peter exercised some special authority-role in the infant Church (it seems obvious from the texts that he did have some such role). Rather, the question we are asking has to do with the nature of that authority: What kind of authority did Peter have, and what was its base?

The classic "Petrine text" is that in Matthew 16:16-18: "You are Peter, and upon this rock. . . ." In explanations of this passage emphasis is usually placed on the reality of the promise, the meaning of the metaphors used ("rock," "binding" and "loosing," etc.), the extension of the promise to Peter's successors. Less often, attention is drawn to earlier verses in the chapter that indicate what might be called the "condition" for Peter's special position. In those early verses Jesus is described as asking his disciples, "Who do men say I am?" to which they reply, in effect, "a great prophet." Jesus then questions the disciples more directly, "Who do *you* say I am?" In answer to this question Simon Peter proclaims his faith in Jesus as the Messiah of Israel. Peter, therefore, will be able to function as a source of stability in a community of believers not only because he possesses a special commission to exercise such a role, but because he possesses faith and can proclaim that faith to others.

This is not a denial of Peter's particular function in the life of the early Christian community, nor is it a claim that Peter's faith in Christ was greater than that of all the other disciples. It is an assertion that without faith Peter could not have carried out his role; that his faith was the root of his act of witnessing to Christ; and that this witness was the heart of his role in the life of the primitive Church. So, before promising Peter this particular position in the community, Jesus demands of him what is needed to fulfill that position: faith that he (Jesus) is the Messiah.

So, too, in the post-Resurrection scene described in John 21:15-19. Again there is question of a special role that Simon Peter is to exercise among the early Christians, a role that is described metaphorically by the words of the risen Christ: "Feed my lambs; feed my sheep." Taking this passage in the context of the entire Gospel of John, one would be justified in saying that Peter is directed to feed the early community with the word of God — something which would require faith on Peter's part. However, the tone of the passage seems to imply more: Peter is to provide for those in the Church with the loving care that is symbolized in the figure of the shepherd and his flock.

Just as in Matthew 16 the protestation of faith by Peter was the prelude to Jesus' promise to him, so in John 21 Jesus demands love from Peter before commanding him to care lovingly for the flock. The risen Christ asks Peter to declare his love for him: "Simon, son of John, do you love me?" By implication, if one truly loves the risen Christ, he will necessarily love those who are Christ's followers and who are therefore dear to Christ.

One must be careful not to read these two texts falsely by concluding that Peter's authority in the early Church depended solely on the level of his faith and love, or by suggesting that Peter deserved the role he had because of the superiority of his faith and love. But it does seem unavoidable to conclude that the kind of authority which Peter did have could only be exercised in faith and in love, and would be exercised effectively in proportion to the depth of his faith and love.

Ministries in the Church

What, then, can one say, on the basis of reflecting on the texts of the New Testament, about the kind of authority that is proper to the Church? First, that the early Church recognized the need for some authority, some definite "offices" with proper functions. Once it became clear that the "second coming" of Jesus was not to occur in the immediate future, the early Christians faced the need to establish structures that would guarantee the unity and stability of the community's life. This they did under the guidance of the Spirit and, at least in the early stages, under the direction of the Apostles.

In the case of the early Church the community to be preserved and fostered was (if one accepts Christian faith) a most unique kind of community. It was a unity of persons formed by a shared faith in the risen Christ, by a shared experience of his presence to them in the gift of his Spirit. Their faith was common, and bound them together precisely because there was only one risen Lord toward whom that faith was directed. The task of preserving and deepening the unity of Christian faith was fundamentally one of bringing the consciousness of Christians into contact with the reality of the risen Christ.

This task, as we know from the New Testament writings, especially from the Acts of the Apostles, comprised two stages: the proclamation of the kerygma and the consequent catechesis of the baptized. The first of these activities was essentially a matter of witnessing to the fact that Jesus of Nazareth had lived, died, and risen, and that he was now Messiah and Lord. Though such proclamation was, mainly, the function of the immediate disciples of Jesus, who had actually experienced this Passover event as it happened, it was also the function of the entire Christian people (and, for that matter, still is). However, there was a special authority that attached to the witness of the Apostles, precisely because of their direct experience. For this reason, the early Church was at pains to preserve the apostolic witness and did so in two ways: through the New Testament writings and through those who succeeded the Apostles and conveyed to a later generation their witness.

Preaching the kerygma was meant to lead to conversion and entry into the Christian community through baptism. Increasing numbers of men and women responded in this way during the early decades of the Christian epoch. With this increase there developed a broader need for instruction, for catechesis, that would explain the implications of Christ's death and resurrection. Here, too, the Apostles played a central role in the early decades, but the need must have arisen almost immediately for others to share in this task. And while some occasions, such as the gathering of a Christian community for prayer and "the breaking of the bread," would have provided a more formal setting for this instruction, a considerable amount of the explanation about Christ's meaning and the nature of Christian faith and life must have been given quite informally.

In the earliest Christian communities (for example, the community established by Paul at Corinth) there was, apparently, a rather broad range of recognized functions, functions which later on ceased to exist or were absorbed into the office we know as the episcopacy. In addition to those who provided for the management of the group or for its temporal needs (the roles that evolved into the offices of bishop, priest, and deacon), there were prophets, teachers, apostles, and those who were gifted with tongues or the interpretation of tongues. And it seems that at least some of these, like the prophets, needed some sort of approval before they could prophesy with authority.

Within a short time, and for a variety of historical reasons, three of these offices (those of bishop, priest, and deacon) absorbed most of the official authority within the Christian community, and the authority of the bishop came to be looked upon as the source of the authority possessed by priests and deacons. Some of the other roles, like that of prophet or teacher, have actually continued in the Church's life throughout the centuries up to our own day, but have had no official recognition or any standing among the Orders in the Church's hierarchical structure. In the ordination ceremony described in the *Apostolic Tradition* of Hippolytus (written about 215), however, we find mention of bishop, priest, deacon, and also of confessors, widows, readers, virgins, subdeacons, and those with the gift of healing.

Historical studies on the origins of Christianity as well as the practical needs of the Church today have brought about a serious reappraisal of ministries within the Christian community. This reappraisal is taking place, not only within the Roman Catholic Church, but in almost every other Christian group. For the moment we have not advanced far enough in this process to make many clear theological or practical judgments, even though the Roman Catholic Church, which had allowed even the diaconate to become nothing more than a stage in a seminarian's advance to the office of priesthood, has now begun the reactivation of this office as a distinct function in the Church's life.

There is, certainly, room for a greater diversity of functions within the Church's life. Or perhaps we should say there is need for the recognition that such diverse functions are actually being exercised and that one or other kind of authority is attached to them. There is a specific role proper to the offices of bishop, priest, and deacon, and a specific authority accompanying each role; but it is not perfectly clear what belongs essentially to each role (the case of the bishop's office is the most critical) and what has become associated with that role through accidental historical accretion.

Whatever authoritative voice belongs to any group or individual in the Christian community, can operate only within the context of faith. Whether it be bishop or priest or teacher or prophet (if there be such), he can legitimately exercise his authority only by clarifying or deepening the faith of his fellow-Christians. His function, whatever position he may occupy, can only be one of witnessing to the reality and to the challenge of the Gospel, or of making more explicit the implications of the Gospel. One cannot legislate faith; one can only witness to the reality of the risen Christ. It is he who demands faith as response to what he says and does.

Authority and Obedience

As we saw earlier, it is in his death and resurrection, that is, in his supreme act of revealing his Father and his total self-gift to men, that Jesus assumed his full authority over men — primarily over those in his Church, but also, through the Church, over all mankind. The resurrection of Christ, however, is a continuing reality in which he still reveals and gives himself. The authority he exerts on men is not, then, just the power of the teaching he gave centuries ago, or the force of his example as the perfect man, or the appeal of his self-sacrifice on behalf of men. Instead, it is the personal power of a man who still communicates to his friends the vision and the wisdom that come from his own unique possession of truth, who still comes in loving concern and presence and invites men and women to respond to the challenge of his love.

Giving himself in this way as the risen Lord, Jesus is the ultimate law of human behavior, the ruler of men's inner dispositions and, as a result, of their external behavior. He is such, at least, for those who accept him in faith. In being law and ruler, the risen Christ resolves totally the seeming opposition between law and freedom. It is his death and resurrection that achieve human freedom, for they overcome the very source of human enslavement: evil in all its forms — sin, fear, and death. In challenging men to respond to his self-giving, the risen Christ provides them with the motive power that they need to overcome fear and self-centeredness and dishonesty, those things that keep them from genuine selfhood and truly personal freedom.

Whatever authority is exercised in Christ's name in the Church must function in this atmosphere of freedom. If the Christian community is to fulfill its role as the sacrament of Christ, as the sign of his continuing redemptive presence among men, it must speak clearly to mankind the liberation that comes to men when they accept the risen Christ in faith and begin to live in response to him. The Church can do this effectively if her own members relate to one another and to life in general with a mature freedom of spirit. Whenever fear or political expediency, rather than free and open acceptance of necessary direction, mark the response to authority in the life of the Church, the Church fails to function as true reflection of Christ and his Spirit.

Obedience in the lives of Christians is meant to be what it was and is in the life of Jesus himself: a grateful acceptance of life as it is given by God the Father. Since that life is one that comes to fulfillment through contact with Christ; since such contact can be achieved only in a community of believers; and since that community of believers, the Church, requires some authority for the unity of its belief and the stability of its existence, the acceptance of legitimate authority in the Church is a part of a person's mature acceptance of life as a gift from Christ and his Father. In Christian life, obedience and gratitude are practically equivalent. The action by which Christians pledge their obedience to the new covenant in faith and hope is the Eucharist, the act of "giving thanks."

This approach to authority and obedience should mark every authority-relationship in the Christian community. While the precise manner of exercising authority will differ in each situation, the basic procedure must be the same in all: Men and women must be brought into contact with the risen Christ, so that in freedom they may come to a deepened faith and thus determine their lives in response to Christ. Which is just another way of saying that authority is exercised in the Church by proclaiming the Gospel. There can be no opposition between law and Gospel in Christianity, for the only authentic law is the Gospel.

Obviously, such use of authority does not automatically guarantee a response of obedience from those to whom the Gospel and its implications are presented. Some, perhaps many, will refuse such response and prefer to follow their own "wisdom." And in such instances, one in authority in the Church can appeal to no sanction other than the intrinsic one of the recalcitrant person's own self-limitation and loss of life and happiness. This is a situation with risk, but a risk which is inevitable in the human condition. Risk is the price of freedom, but it is also the occasion for developing personal maturity. It is such freedom and maturity, both for individual Christians and for the Church as a community, that the New Testament literature envisages.

Reflection on this literature provides us with an insight into what authority and law, obedience and freedom, are meant to be in the life of the Church. By itself such reflection cannot give all the knowledge that we need to appraise the authority of the Church as we experience it today; we must also undertake a careful study of the historical evolution of offices within the life of the Church, for the Spirit does not cease to guide and direct the development of the Christian community. What this reflection does provide are the fundamental guidelines for evaluating the developments of history and the situation in which we now find ourselves, so that we can more fully bring the community existence of the Church into conformity with the Gospel.

The realization within the Church's life of authority exercised in faith and love, and of obedience exercised in freedom and gratitude, is not just a matter of the Church's own internal well-being. In living this way, structured but free, the Christian community is meant to be a sign of hope to all human societies, hope that they can also exist with just exercise of law and authority. To the extent that the Church brings the ideal of authority for the sake of freedom into the patterns of man's social existence, she will have shared in Christ's task of liberating mankind.

CHAPTER TWO

Mission to the World

FOR MORE THAN a century Christianity has had to live with a radical and clearly-voiced challenge to its very reason for existence. Marx's charge that religion is the "opium of the people," a deterrent rather than an aid to human development; and Nietzsche's proclamation that "God is dead" and man is therefore free to attain his true stature, are but two of the best-known formulations of this challenge.

Actually, the challenge runs very deep, and for centuries has been gaining momentum as modern man increasingly gained a mastery of the forces of nature and life. In our own day, as mankind stands on the threshhold of unprecedented human achievement, when technology and communications media and research in the life-sciences give promise of a "new age," secularity is laying claim to being the only viable "religion." At a time when the human race seems to have achieved a new maturity, in a "world come of age," is it not appropriate that men should shoulder their own problems and solve them, instead of hoping that some "God" will intervene to take care of them?

It must be admitted that institutionalized Christianity has often enough laid itself open to the charge of irrelevance. Instead of encouraging and supporting those developments which have brought increased freedom and human betterment, the Christian Churches have often found themselves allied with colonialism and autocratic governments, supporting outmoded social and political structures, viewing the advance of scientific knowledge with suspicion and even fear.

The Gospel, which the New Testament literature describes

as something startlingly new, has seemed to many moderns as old and out-of-date. The Church, whose very being is eschatological, that is, future-oriented, has given the impression of having little, if anything, to contribute to man's future. Perhaps, suggest some, the Church has served her historical function and should quietly go out of existence.

Christians who do not accept this pessimistic judgment about the future of the Church are faced with the need to explain the purpose of Christianity in the contemporary world. What is the Church meant to accomplish? Does she exist in order to stand apart from the secular progress of mankind and to insist that man's fulfillment can come only in "the world beyond"? Is her purpose to help men "save their souls," and to do so precisely by helping to preserve them from the evil forces of "the world"? These are not rhetorical questions to which one can quickly give a negative answer, hoping thereby to put the Church's activity in a more contemporary and acceptable light.

To give an unqualified "no" to these questions would be to betray some elements of the New Testament teaching. In the temptation in the desert, Jesus is described as refusing earthly wealth and power as a means of fulfilling his messianic role (Mt. 4:8-10). The Sermon on the Mount certainly advocates something less than total dedication to the pursuit of temporal goods: "the Gentiles seek all these things" (Mt. 6:32). And the Gospel of John, in its seventeenth chapter, depicts Jesus praying to his Father to preserve his disciples from "the world" (Jn. 17:15).

There is a certain tension in New Testament teaching on this point: in some opposition to the texts that speak warningly of "the world" are others, like John 3:16 ("God so loved the world . . ."), which view the world as touched and transformed by the saving mystery of the Incarnation.

Vatican II, especially in its Pastoral Constitution on the Church in the Modern World, has clearly directed Catholic thought and life to an emphasis on the present world. Without in any way denying the need for human salvation through the death and resurrection of Christ, or denying the inability of purely human effort to achieve the destiny of mankind, the Council has directed the life of the Church "outward." As Christ himself came to work for others, the Christian community exists for the sake of men; the Church's mission is to the world in which she finds herself situated. If Christians are to implement the mission of Christ which they share, they cannot refuse identification and involvement with their contemporaries.

Central to the Council's stress on Christian involvement in the world is its recognition of the status and role of the layman. Relegated for many centuries to "second-class citizenship" in the Church, the laity have once more regained their rightful place in the Church's life, though it will unquestionably take some decades for this recognition to be translated into the practicalities of the Church's existence. It would be difficult to exaggerate the importance of this shift of emphasis. A clericalized Church, in which Christian apostolic activity was the special prerogative of an ordained caste, would be utterly incapable of relating to the needs and potential of the contemporary world. Only the laity — men and women who share in human society as scientists and businessmen and artists and parents and citizens — can bring Christianity into immediate conjunction with the evolving patterns of today's world.

This conclusion raises many questions, obviously, about the role of the clergy in the world of today and tomorrow, but it is not our intent to face these questions at this point. Our purpose is to study the mission of the Christian community as a whole, the entire "people of God," and to do so in the light of Christianity's origins as we find them reflected in the New Testament literature.

Given the immense and complex problems of contemporary society and the obvious need to find a solution to those problems as quickly as possible, it may seem a vain and unrealistic effort to examine the experience and viewpoint of early Christianity for help in this regard. That would be true, if one were to look in the New Testament books for specific answers to the questions that modern man faces. On the other hand, what is needed by Christians as they confront the task of improving human life is a basic viewpoint, a set of principles and values, that can guide them as they move into new and unprecedented situations. This, perhaps, the New Testament can provide.

The World and the Kingdom

As soon as one does approach the New Testament writings with this objective in mind a difficulty arises: If one takes seriously the kinds of Christian activity advocated by Vatican II's Constitution on the Church and the Modern World (or, parallel to it, the social encyclicals of recent popes), it is clear that what is called for is the basic humanization of society on a worldwide scale. Such a perspective seems far from the thought of the early decades of Christianity. Existing in small and scattered communities, the early Christians were hardly in a position to think about becoming a major social influence.

As one first approaches the New Testament teaching there seems to be little, if any, hope of agreement between the Gospel of the risen Christ and the secular hopes and ambitions of contemporary man. From beginning to end, the books of the New Testament are interested in the establishment of "the kingdom of God"; this kingdom is plainly not an earthly realm.

Furthermore, it would be easy to read the texts that speak of "the kingdom of God" and understand them to refer to an other-worldly situation. This is particularly true of Matthew's Gospel, where the term "kingdom of heaven" is commonly used as an equivalent for "kingdom of God." Yet to place the kingdom about which Jesus and the early Church spoke apart from man's life on this earth does not seem to agree with certain key passages, like that which describes Jesus' healing of the paralytic (Mt. 9:1-8).

All three synoptic Gospels relate this scene; all three place

it early in the public ministry of Jesus; and in all three it is the
first mention of conflict between Jesus and the scribes and
Pharisees. The focus of the conflict is Jesus' claim to have the
authority to forgive sins, a claim which the Jewish leaders see
as blasphemous. What is particularly significant in the passage, at least in the light of our present question, is the statement ". . . the Son of man has authority *on earth* to forgive
sins."

It seems quite clear that the background of this statement
is the seventh chapter of the book of Daniel, which describes
the triumph of the faithful Jews over their earthly oppressors
and the future rule and glory of the chosen people. This future "kingdom of the saints" is placed in a heavenly context,
apparently beyond history and this earth. At one point in the
passage, this future kingdom of the saints is personified by
the figure of "one like a son of man"; to this figure there is
given dominion, and glory, and kingdom.

It seems evident that Jesus, in the Gospel scene we are
studying, lays claim to being this "son of man," the realization of the idea of the kingdom of the saints, the fulfillment of
Judaism. However, the exercise of the authority proper to this
"son of man" is located on earth and in history. When we recall that the Gospel writers, drawing from the early Christian
traditions about Jesus, are already aware of his death and resurrection and might therefore be expected to stress the "heavenly" character of Jesus' authority as the risen Lord, it seems
quite important that this passage describes Jesus as already
exercising his power during his earthly career. The fact that
Jesus' authority is not *of* this world (that is, not derived from
ordinary sources of political or social power) does not pre-
clude the possibility of its being exercised *in* this world.

This same distinction seems to be applicable to the seventeenth chapter of John's Gospel, where Jesus prays that his
disciples be kept free from evil influences in the world but not
that they should be removed from the world. Though his disciples are in the world, as is Jesus himself in his public ministry, they are no more of the world than he is. While they

must remain in some sense free from identification with the world, they are still sent into the world to bear witness to the truth. "They are not of the world, even as I am not of the world. Sanctify them in the truth; thy word is truth. As thou didst send me into the world, so I have sent them into the world" (Jn. 17:16-18).

Jesus' mission, then, is one of coming into the world in order to establish the kingdom of his Father, a kingdom different from earthly kingdoms. A careful examination of the texts that speak of "the kingdom of God" indicates that one must not too quickly and readily identify this "kingdom" with a given social structure, not even the social structure of the Church. "Kingdom of God" has a more dynamic meaning and refers essentially to the Father's rule over the lives and actions of men.

As one puzzles over the passages that speak of the kingdom of the Father (which is also the kingdom of Christ, for he is the heir with whom the Father shares his rule) it becomes clear that the point at issue is a correct understanding of what is often called "divine providence." Since the Father of Christ is identified by Christian faith as God in the fullest sense — eternal, almighty, infinite — his rule over creation is, from one point of view, absolute and inescapable. Nothing is, except he knows and wills it. Yet this acceptance of creative omnipotence is combined with an unmistakable acceptance of human freedom. Why else would Jesus have the mission of winning the kingdom for his Father? Jesus' work was and is that of converting men to his Father, challenging them to a free response to his Father's love.

But Jesus' work is also one of opposing and overcoming the forces of evil. Mysterious though evil is, there is no possibility of denying its reality or its strange attraction for men. And if God will act in human affairs with genuine regard for man's power of choice — which he does — men have the frightening ability to choose evil rather than God. Yet, the Father who creates men in love and who "does not desire the death of the sinner" sends his own Son into human history with the mission of winning the kingdom — men's hearts — which rightfully belongs to him.

This view of the manner in which divine providence operates goes beyond the perspective of Old Testament thought in building upon it. By the time of the Babylonian exile and the high point of charismatic prophecy in Israel, the guidance of human history is seen to consist in an interplay between Yahweh's "call" to man and man's response to that call. Deuteronomic theology placed too strong an emphasis on the human determinant: if a man performs good actions, he is blessed; if he does evil, he is punished. The book of Job is a challenge to the adequacy of this Deuteronomic view, and Deutero-Isaiah expresses the transcendence of Yahweh's activity: "For my thoughts are not your thoughts, neither are your ways my ways, says the Lord" (Is. 55:8). Still, human freedom is an indispensable element. Yahweh does not save men against their will, but sends the prophets to preach conversion.

When we turn to the New Testament writings, we notice that all four Gospels begin with a mention of John the Baptist's role as herald of the Gospel. His prophetic message stands in continuity with Old Testament prophetism: "Be converted, for the kingdom of God is at hand." When Jesus appears on the scene to begin his work of establishing the Father's kingdom, he preaches the same message. Indeed, Jesus' public teaching seems to have been almost totally an explanation of the Father's kingdom. The early Church incorporated that teaching into its catechesis, so that believers might better understand Christ's death and resurrection, which was the definitive establishment of that kingdom.

The Hour of the Lord

Old Testament reflection about the establishment of God's rule in history centered, at least from Amos onward, on the anticipated "day of the Lord." Prophetic descriptions of this "day" alternate between predictions of doom and punishment and promises of restoration and glory for Israel. While Yahweh's action is the focus of attention in these prophetic passages, human freedom is also prominent. The prophetic exhortation to conversion implies the possibility of doom being averted if Israel will turn from her sinful ways. Human choice by itself, however, is not the ultimate determinant. Even sinful Israel will not be abandoned by Yahweh. He will punish in order to win back his people, but in his mercy he will forgive and restore them.

Early Christianity saw the expectations of this salvific "day of the Lord" fulfilled in Jesus of Nazareth. From one point of view, this new day dawned with the Incarnation, and the entire career of Jesus manifests the saving action of the Father. However, full and definitive salvation comes with Jesus' death and resurrection; this is "his hour" (Jn 13:1). Jesus' Passover from this life to the new life of resurrection is his entry into the ultimate promised land; this is the new Exodus in which a new Israel is constituted; this is Jesus' claim to the kingdom of his Father in which he shares.

John's Gospel, in particular, stresses the theme of "the hour" of Jesus. In its description of the marriage feast of Cana and the changing of the water into wine, "the first sign that Jesus did," the Gospel draws attention to the fact that this was not yet Jesus' full manifestation of himself, for "my hour has not yet come" (Jn. 2:4). When, however, the Gospel narrative introduces the scene of the Last Supper, the first stage in Jesus' Passover act, it mentions that Jesus "knew his hour had come" and gathered his disciples together for the supper (Jn. 13:1).

Luke's Gospel does essentially the same thing, for it describes the Supper as the establishment of the kingdom. Not only is the giving of his body under the appearances of bread seen as a sign of the coming of the kingdom, but after the meal Jesus is described as bestowing the kingdom on his followers: "as my Father has appointed a kingdom for me, so do I appoint for you that you may eat and drink at my table in my kingdom" (Lk. 22:29).

But if Jesus' Passover is his hour, it is also the hour of the power of evil. In the perspective of the New Testament writers, the death and resurrection of Jesus is the supreme conflict between God and evil. The essential character of sin is revealed in the attempt to destroy Jesus, who is the greatest manifestation of the Father's redeeming love. Evil would, if it could, remove God's love from human history and so destroy the possibility of men reaching their destiny. Yet in the death of Jesus evil overreaches itself and paradoxically provides the context for divine love's ultimate manifestation. In his public teaching Jesus had once said, "Greater love has no man than this, that a man lay down his life for his friends" (Jn. 15:13). Now in his gift to men through death and resurrection, the gift of himself as source of new life, he proves the depth of his own love and sacramentalizes the love of his Father.

At the root of Jesus' triumph over the forces of evil lies his human act of love and free decision. There is nothing magical about the manner in which his death destroyed forever the power of sin. This death, freely accepted out of love for his Father and for men, was a total gift of self to others and, therefore, a direct contradiction of sin, which is a denial of self to others. The power of his death is the power of personal love, human and divine. This is the power proper to the kingdom of God, the power by which both Christ and his Father rule the hearts and lives of those who will accept this love.

Unquestionably, the faith of the early Christians in the power of Christ's death and resurrection, their belief that this event marked the turning point in human history and that it provided the answer to the human condition, is difficult to accept. Paul himself recognized (as he mentions to the Corinthian community) that this belief was largely unacceptable to both Jew and Greek in his day (1 Cor. 1:23). For those who believe, however, Christ's Passover into risen life is the key to the riddle of human life; it is the source of true wisdom.

Christ's apparent defeat on Calvary was actually his moment of victory. In being obedient, even to death, he becomes "the Lord," the head and ruler of mankind and of the entire created universe (Phil. 2). In confronting hatred and hostile dishonesty, yet never ceasing to love or to witness to truth, Jesus absorbed and overcame evil. In so doing he exercised fully his saving role. As the risen Lord, he can carry on the redeeming work of his Father by imparting his own Spirit to men.

The full actuality of "divine providence" is thus revealed in Jesus' death and resurrection. God the Father guides human history by sending his own Son, so that, become man, he can lead his fellow-men to their destiny. This Son-become-man, Jesus of Nazareth, has in essence performed this mission by blazing the trail into new life through his own death and resurrection. But each generation of men and women needs to be guided along this path toward true life. To accomplish this task, the risen Lord abides with men, especially with those in the Christian community, so that through them he can continue his mission.

It is in this fashion that the kingdom of God is meant to be established as human history unfolds. Centrally effective though the death of Jesus and his passage into new life are, it would be a mistake to think that Christ at that point had finished his mission. It is with his role as risen Lord that he gains the full power to gain men in freedom and love for his Father. "My Father works until now and I work."

The Messianic Mission

When the early Church in her kerygma proclaimed Jesus as "Lord," she joined to that title the name "Messiah." In attributing messiahship to Jesus, the early Christians were explicitly linking the mission of Jesus to Old Testament understandings of kingship, particularly to the messianic idealization of Davidic kingship. The application of the name "Christ" ("Messiah") to Jesus represented a radical transposition of Old Testament thought. Before examining this development, we must study the extent to which Jesus' mission stands in continuity with Israel's stated hopes for an ideal king. In doing this we may gain some insight into the manner in which the mission of Christ and of the Church is relevant to the social structures of human life.

One of the earliest messianic passages is contained in the ninth chapter of Isaiah: "For to us a child is born, to us a son is given . . ." (v. 6). Perhaps originally used with reference to Hezekiah (and therefore to be linked with the famous "Emmanuel" passage in Isaiah 7), the text describes the ideal king. His rule will achieve the longed-for lasting peace, because he will administer his charge with justice and truth. Grounded in the righteousness of his rule, his kingdom will enjoy stability and permanence. Though the king idealized in this passage is obviously thought of as a powerful ruler, there is no mention of his power deriving either from military strength or from wealth. His strength will lie in his personal qualifications and integrity.

Much the same picture is provided by the parallel passage found two chapters later (Isaiah 11:1-5). Here again the power of the king will derive from the justice of his decrees, from the righteousness of his judgment. He will effectively overcome the wicked and will act as a safeguard for the poor. In all things he will be guided by truth and will not be misled by false appearances.

What the passage stresses, however, is the idealized king's possession of the "spirit of the Lord." This spirit will give him the gifts of wisdom and understanding, counsel and might and knowledge. And these gifts will be rooted in the gift of fear of the Lord, that reverence and acknowledgement of Yahweh which preserves the king from the temptation to think that he, rather than Yahweh, is the savior of the people. The word of judgment by which the ideal king will rule will be guided, then, by the same "spirit of the Lord" which came to the great prophets in their prophetic vocation.

We might glance briefly at a third passage, because, like the two texts just discussed, it exercised a strong influence on the New Testament description of Jesus. It is found in chapter thirty-four of Ezekiel, which begins by telling of the way in which Yahweh himself will be the shepherd of his people. Taking pity on his flock which has been scattered (through the exiles) because of the rapacity and treachery of its appointed shepherds, Yahweh promises to come and to gather together the lost sheep and to lead them to good pasture. Applying this same image to the expected Messiah, the passage continues: "And I will set up over them one shepherd, my servant David, and he shall feed them: he shall feed them and be their shepherd" (Ezek. 34:23).

Here the emphasis is clearly laid on the Messiah's function of providing for the needs of the people, particularly of the poor and weak who had previously been exploited. Moreover, he is to rule with gentleness and concern, in contrast to the unfaithful shepherds who are accused earlier in the chapter. Finally, he must provide for the continued unity of the people, not allowing the sheep to be scattered.

Israel's messianic expectations, as these three passages indicate, were firmly linked to the political and social structures of the people's life. Even though idealized, the awaited Messiah was still seen as an earthly monarch, operating through the processes of civil government. Fulfillment of the messianic promises would mean the advent of a human society which would respect and foster the dignity and welfare of all human beings.

When the early Christians acclaimed Jesus as the Messiah, they were well aware of this background of Old Testament thought. They took pains, in fact, to relate the life and actions of Jesus, especially his death and resurrection, to these Old Testament anticipations. Yet they were also aware that the very notion of a Messiah had undergone a radical revision through its realization in Jesus. Jesus was indeed the Messiah of Israel — the faith of early Christianity is unmistakable on this point — but he had fulfilled the messianic promises in a way that no one could have anticipated. He was a king, but his kingship was quite other than that with which his contemporaries were familiar.

From one point of view, the nonpolitical character of

Jesus' claim to be Messiah should not have been too great a shock to Jewish minds in his day. In applying kingship to the religious sphere, especially in applying it to Yahweh himself and calling him "king," Old Testament thought had already been forced to make some adjustments in the notion of kingship. This in turn had forced a reappraisal of kingship as a political institution in Israelitic society, for the king was to be the representative of Yahweh, who alone was the ultimate ruler of the people. As the biblical record of kingship in Israel clearly attests, this necessity created a continuing problem that was resolved only when kingship vanished from Israel's life. The kings, understandably enough, tended to forget the special character of their office and acted much as any other ancient ruler. They were caught up in political, economic, and military ways of thinking about Israel's welfare, with the result that the religious perspective was often lost. Even worse, the religion of Israel was at times subordinated to the political advantage of the kings, as if Yahweh were primarily the king's protector.

What happened to safeguard the true nature of Old Testament religion and to prevent its absorption into increasingly secular social institutions was the rise of charismatic prophecy. Through the word of the prophet, Yahweh manifested his will to the people, often enough in opposition to the words of the king and his supporters. The great prophets did not espouse the elimination of kingship, and even seem to have acknowledged the practical need for some such guidance of society, for they repeatedly directed their oracles to the king himself in the hope that he would mend his ways. Besides, it was the prophetic movement that did much to develop and cherish the anticipation of a great future king, the Messiah.

When one asks whether it was kingship or prophecy that most authentically guided Israelitic society according to the will of Yahweh, the answer of the Old Testament literature is clear: the prophets. If Old Testament history is viewed as a process in which God gradually established his kingdom, it would follow that the charismatic prophet was a more effective agent of Yahweh's kingship than the Davidic dynasty.

In the New Testament description of Jesus, the prophetic emphasis outweighs the kingly, at least if one understands "kingly" in ordinary terms. Particularly in the Gospel narration of the public ministry, the activity of Jesus is almost totally that of a prophet, and it was as prophet that the people acclaimed him. Yet, in a progression of insight that is not perfectly clear, the immediate disciples of Jesus began to realize that this new prophet was the awaited Messiah.

No sooner had they come to acknowledge his messianic identity, than Jesus began to readjust their understanding of the Messiah. He did this by predicting his suffering and death in Jerusalem, a happening that no doubt seemed to his disciples utterly out of keeping with the establishment of a kingdom. Along with their Jewish contemporaries, the disciples of Jesus looked forward to a messianic figure who would reestablish the temporal power of the Jewish people and inaugurate an epoch of earthly prosperity. Only the death and resurrection of Jesus was able to dispel this notion and open to the early Christians a new and nonpolitical understanding of the kingship of Jesus.

Two factors were of key importance in the transformation of messianic hopes that Jesus effected. First, there was the fact that he fulfilled in himself not only the figure of the Messiah, but also the Old Testament ideals connected with the "suffering Servant" of Isaiah 52-53, with Daniel's figure of "the Son of man," with Solomon as the epitome of wisdom, and with Moses as lawgiver. As we pointed out earlier, by virtue of their convergence in Jesus, each of these Old Testament notions forced a reinterpretation of the others. In a special way, Jesus' claim to be the "suffering Servant" and his verification of that claim through his death forced a basic reconsideration of his messiahship.

Second, Jesus' teaching about the identity of his Father, and about the manner in which his Father ruled, reiterated and deepened the Old Testament insights into the "spiritual" nature of God's influence on human affairs. The kingdom that Jesus announced as imminent and that he worked to establish was the kingdom of his Father, his Father's rule over men's lives. The parables, so often beginning "The kingdom of heaven is like . . . ," are essentially descriptions of the Father, of the Father's attitude to men, of the Father's purpose and manner of acting in the world. Jesus is the emissary of this Father, the heir who has been sent into the world to lay claim to the kingdom for his Father. And if he is to share kingly power with his Father, his own rule as Messiah and Lord cannot be a different kind of rule than that exercised by his Father.

This manner of ruling, as we saw, is one of influencing men through the gift of self in love. Jesus already exerted this divinely royal power during his earthly ministry; exercised it fully in his death and resurrection; and continues to rule as Messiah and Lord by communicating to men the Spirit he shares with his Father. To the extent that men and women open themselves to the gift of his Spirit, they will discover and accept their own relationship to the Father, and their love for this Father will be the ruling influence in their lives. Such is the kingdom of God.

Though Jesus in his death and resurrection has passed into a way of human existence where he is no longer sensibly present, he still remains present to human history and carries on the mission of establishing his Father's rule. This he does through the instrumentality of the Christian community which he instituted, and to which he transmitted his own Spirit.

Church and Evangelization

When one reads the books of the New Testament, particularly the Acts and the letters of Paul, he realizes that the term "institution of the Church" must be used cautiously. The very term, which is not itself found in the New Testament literature, tends to give the impression that Jesus himself established the institutionalized structures that we have learned to associate with the Church's existence. This in turn can lead to a misunderstanding of the kind of kingdom that Christ established in his death and resurrection.

It is, of course, true that "Christ instituted the Church," provided one understands that statement in the light of the evidence provided by the New Testament and other early Christian writings. Christianity took its origin in dynamic fashion from the event of Christ's death and resurrection, and it continues in existence because it continues to draw from that same source of vitality and human community. What Christ did as the heart of his "instituting the Church" was to pass into that situation of risen life and power in which he can be the source of the Christian community's life and unity.

This is not to say that the public ministry of Jesus played no part in the beginning of Christianity. Not only did Jesus in those months provide an insight into his Father and into human life from which all generations of Christians have drawn, he also gathered around him the small group of followers who would form the nucleus of the first Christian communities. All this was, however, by way of preparation. The Church is essentially a community of believers in the resurrection of Christ; it was the resurrection that gave them this principle of unity in faith.

Moreover, the event of Christ's death and resurrection contains as an integral element the pentecostal sending of the Spirit. Raised to full human sharing in the power and glory of his Father, Jesus shares with his followers that Spirit in which he finds his human fulfillment. This sending of the Spirit is not a once-for-all occurrence that takes place only on "Pentecost Sunday" (Acts 2). The Acts describes the giving of the Spirit to the community as a recurring reality.

The Spirit of the risen Christ is the source of the early Church's corporate existence and social vitality; her members are bound to one another as Christians because they share this same Spirit. It is this Spirit who guides the development of their faith and their understanding of what it is that happened in the Christ-event: "But the Counselor, the Holy Spirit, whom the Father will send in my name, he will teach you all things, and bring to your remembrance all that I have said to you" (Jn. 14:26).

From the Spirit who dwelt with them came the various gifts — the charisms — that helped shape the community existence of the infant Church: charisms of prophecy, of tongues, of teaching, of governing. Gradually, some of these charismatic expressions of Christ's Spirit developed into the established "offices" (*episkopos, presbyteros, diakonos*) that formed the institutionalized structure of the Church. Some stable structuring of the Christian community was needed if it was to remain united and operate effectively, but the early Christians saw the emergence of these structures as resulting from something more than human awareness of this need and human decision to provide for the need. For them, the externally visible forms of their community existence were the expression of the unifying and vitalizing action of the Spirit.

The Spirit did not work in the Christian community solely for the good of that group of believers. Christ had died and risen for all men, and the Spirit was sent into the Church so that this universal redemption might be accomplished. The presence of the Spirit to the early Christians was the first stage of Jesus' "mission," but that mission extended beyond the Christian community itself and was meant to be accomplished through the instrumentality of Christians. This is another way of saying that Christianity, from its beginnings, was entrusted with the mission of continuing Christ's redeeming work.

Early Christianity is explicit in its faith that the missionary effort in which it was engaged was rooted in the "urgings" of the Holy Spirit. This claim gains credence as one reflects on the context out of which Christianity emerged. Most of the earliest Christians were Jewish, and in its beginnings the Christian community may very well have been looked on as another Jewish sect. Besides, the New Testament writings leave no doubt that these early followers of Christ considered themselves the continuation and fulfillment of Old Testament Israel. But Judaism was not a missionary religion; converts to

Jewish faith were admitted into the people, but there was no movement to go out to Gentiles and convert them.

The missionary impulse of early Christianity is, then, something new and distinctive in the ancient world. There were historical factors, such as the mounting opposition of the Jewish leadership in Jerusalem, that contributed to the conviction of these first Christians that they were meant to bring the Gospel of the risen Christ to "the ends of the earth." But these factors were secondary, and only confirmed the basic missionary thrust that came from the Spirit.

One of the most striking passages in this regard is the one that describes the source of Paul's mission to the Mediterranean world. The setting is the Christian community at Antioch, where Paul was staying at that time.

> While they [the Christians at Antioch] were worshipping the Lord and fasting, the Holy Spirit said, "Set apart for me Barnabas and Saul for the work to which I have called them." Then after praying and fasting they laid their hands on them and sent them off (Acts 13:2-3).

While Paul's missionary endeavors were the most extensive and the most famous in the infant Church, he was not alone in this work of evangelization. Christian communities sprang up rapidly throughout the Greco-Roman world, and there are some ancient Christian traditions (not recorded in the New Testament) that Apostles ranged as far west as Spain and as far east as India in their preaching of the Gospel. Whatever may have been the actual extent of this early missionary effort, the infant Church was convinced that she had a mission. This is clearly expressed in the final verses of Matthew's Gospel (Mt. 28:18-20). There the risen Jesus, just before the mystery of his ascension, gives his followers their commission: "Go therefore and make disciples of all nations. . . ."

From this same passage, as well as from Acts and Paul's letters, we can see how the early Christians understood the nature of their mission. Fundamentally they were to preach the Gospel, the "good news" of the advent of God's kingdom in the resurrection of Jesus. They themselves had been privileged to experience the saving event of Christ's Passover; now they were sent to witness to this event before all men.

Having preached this Gospel, and thereby having led men to conversion and acceptance of this saving news, they were to introduce them into the community's life and into union with Christ through the initiating ritual of baptism. This ritual would give expression to the faith which the Gospel was meant to elicit from men, for they were to baptize "in the name of the Father, and of the Son, and of the Holy Spirit." Thereafter, they were to instruct men in that new way of life which Christ had brought to men: "teaching them to observe all that I have commanded you . . ." (Mt. 28:20).

It would seem, then, that the early Christians saw their mission as essentially prophetic. They were to speak for Christ, leading men to conversion so that they would then acknowledge "the Father of our Lord, Jesus Christ." The Spirit who impelled and guided them in this mission was the Spirit of prophecy, who had worked in the great charismatic prophets of Israel and in Jesus' own prophetic ministry. This is the mentality reflected in Acts 2, where the event of Pentecost is seen as the fulfillment of Joel's prophecy that in the "day of the Lord" the Spirit of prophecy would be given to the entire people.

In the view of early Christianity and in the teaching of the New Testament, the Christian community does have a lasting and worldwide mission. Through the preaching of the Gospel, it is to lead men to the Father through Christ and his Spirit, and in this way establish the kingdom of God, his rule over men in love and freedom.

The Mission of the Christian Community

But all this raises again the question with which we began our discussion: Christianity's "solution" to human life, as we find it stated in the New Testament writings, seems to be strictly religious and "otherworldly." At first glance, at least, it does not seem to be able to speak to the grave and complex problems of our contemporary world. The Gospel provides the hope of a new life beyond the barrier of death, but does it provide hope of overcoming the poverty and injustice and oppression that blight the lives of most men and women today? In our present world-situation, with its mixture of fearful threats and unprecedented possibilities for good, does the message of the New Testament and the faith of the Christian Church have anything to offer as a means of building a better life for mankind?

It does seem that one can give an affirmative answer to these questions, even though Christian faith still maintains that a complete solution will not be achieved in this world, that the fullness of life as destined for men can come only in passage through death. Reflection on the content of New Testament faith does give us justification for saying that the mission of the Church is relevant, that Christianity has something of radical importance to offer men today, for the task of building the city of man is at least part of the task of establishing the kingdom of God. What, then, is the Christian community meant to do?

1. Christians, by preaching the Gospel of Christ, are meant to *alter men's vision of life.* The very horizons within which human beings see their lives and destinies cast are broadened immeasurably if one accepts the reality of Jesus' resurrection and of men's share in this new, risen life. Death itself takes on a radically different meaning than it would have without the hope of passing into a new life of fulfillment and happiness beyond — and the manner in which men view life is deeply affected by the manner in which they view death.

Again, the way in which men and women live, make their decisions, develop their cultures, strive for certain goals, is controlled by the notion they have of "man." Ideas shape the world, and the idea of man is of key importance. If man is looked upon as a truly free being, dignified by the reality of the Incarnation, transformed in his personal potential and experience by a loving relationship to God, this view should have important consequences.

The history of Old Testament Israel was different than it otherwise would have been — it became a "salvation history" — because that people believed in the merciful and guiding presence of Yahweh. Christian faith builds upon this experience and goes beyond it, maintaining that Jesus of Nazareth was Emmanuel, God-with-us, and that he still remains present and active in our history as the risen Lord. If this faith of Christianity be true, human life, in this world and beyond, is a partnership, a community, that involves God and men in a genuine personal relationship. Any fatalistic view of human existence is challenged in its roots by such an understanding of the forces that operate in man's life.

From the beginning of Christianity, the preaching of the Gospel has been seen as a process of bringing hope to men. The Gospel is "the good news" because it holds out to men the expectation of bettering the human condition, because it speaks of a power — the risen Lord and his Spirit — that is able to overcome the evils that afflict and demean man, because it speaks of that power as not only triumphing over evil in some "end time" but as already working within men to change the world.

Though it is realistic in facing the ills and problems of human life and the difficulty of human progress, for it deals head-on with the facts of death and sin, the Gospel of Christ is basically optimistic and positive in its perspective. The very fact that it is a call to "conversion" reflects the view that men can change from what is less appropriate to their human dignity to what more befits persons. It requires little reflection to see what impact such an understanding of human life could and should have on the evolution of human society and the betterment of human life.

It would be a mistake, however, to understand what we have been saying as if the Gospel was only a collection of ideas, a series of doctrines, about man's life on this earth. One can formulate such Christian doctrines, and it is probably helpful to do so. Ideas that are formulated in this more precise fashion have considerable power to influence man's individual and social existence. But ideas are most effective socially when they are given expression in ideals, in "heroes" who embody these understandings, in symbols that touch not only the intellectual level of man but his emotional and affective responses as well.

This is the importance of the fact that the Gospel of Christianity is not just a message; it is a person, the risen Christ. For those who accept him in faith, he is the embodiment of what it truly means to be human. Having pledged himself irrevocably, through his death and resurrection, to "being for men," he is the source of Christian hope, he is the living sacrament of divine fidelity. Present and active in the lives of men, he leads them toward increased human freedom and peace and community.

2. Christianity is *a wisdom,* a way of life. From a generic point of view, this is not distinctive of Christianity, for every religion lays claim to being a way of life. What is distinctive about the claim of Christianity is its contention that the Christ who is its object of faith is himself incarnated divine wisdom. He embodies in his own human outlook and activity a wisdom that is human but that draws immediately from the wisdom of God.

Any human culture or society is itself the expression of "a wisdom"; it is what it is because the men and women it involves cherish one set of values rather than another. People spend their energy and time and resources to attain those goals they value. The context of human living that results from such effort is a direct index to the value-system of a given society. In a nation like the United States today, one can gain great insight into the attitudes and motivations of people by examining the advertising to which they are exposed, for such advertising appeals to the values which operate in people's decisions.

It does not require much imagination to foresee how deeply a society (or human society as a whole) would be altered, if the basic values of people were changed. If peace rather than power, justice rather than affluence, brotherhood rather than prejudice, freedom rather than comfort, were the values cherished by men today, the world in which we live would be a far different and better place. As things are, there is often lip-service paid to goals like peace and justice, but the men and women who truly work toward these goals at the expense of their own personal leisure and political power and financial gain are often considered "impractical and idealistic." In other words, they lack practical wisdom.

Christianity, like the Old Testament Israel before it, does claim to have a wisdom that touches the practicalities of human life. In fact, the word "wisdom" in its biblical usage refers to practical human prudence rather than to some abstract and esoteric knowledge. In both Israel and early Christianity, as we can see from the literature they produced, the wise man was the one who truly understood what human life was all about, the one who knew the secret to living a successful life despite the dangers and difficulties that beset mankind, the one who had discovered how to reach true peace and joy.

Old Testament thought, as it reflected on the true nature of wisdom, idealized the figure of Solomon and made him the epitome of wisdom. New Testament thought sees Jesus of Nazareth as surpassing even Solomon. Jesus is the very wisdom of God become man, so that he can teach men the path to happiness. In the Gospel of John the teaching of Jesus is clearly described as aiming at the achievement of men's happiness. In the "last discourse" (Jn. 13-17), this is a recurrent theme: "These things I have spoken to you, that my joy may be in you, and that your joy may be full." "I have said this to you, that in me you may have peace."

Though the wisdom espoused by Christianity is often rejected as unrealistic, or the values it cherishes placed second to other goals that men desire, the value-system of the Gospel may be particularly significant in our present world-situation. Perhaps nothing is a more fundamental value-judgment in the teaching of Jesus than the priority of human persons over material goods. This is the essential meaning of Christian poverty: Human persons are never to be subordinated to things, and each man must guard against a possessiveness that would destroy his personal freedom and integrity. Moreover, each man and woman who accepts the Gospel of Christ must bear the responsibility of seeing that other humans are not exploited by a society that places economic growth before justice.

Christianity is not alone in insisting on the unique value of the human person. Other religions like Judaism and Islamism teach the dignity of man, and many devoted "humanists" who are (at least explicitly) without religion give their lives to advancing the cause of human freedom and equality. But, if Christianity is right in its faith in the Incarnation, it can point to a basis of human personal greatness beyond anything otherwise imaginable.

3. Christians are meant to *bring love into men's lives* — not just their own love but the love of Christ and of his Father. Here, too, the Christian community cannot lay claim to a monopoly. Many other men and women bring love into the lives of their fellow-men, and that love is in a profound (though perhaps unrecognized) way a manifestation of God's love for men. What Christians are able to do, because of their faith in the identity of Jesus as the Father's own Son who is sent into human history because of that Father's love for men, is to speak more explicitly about the reality of God's love for all men.

Obviously, it is not enough for Christians to talk about love. They are themselves to give their love to people, regardless of social status or ethnic background or cultural differences. Even the hostility that others might manifest does not excuse Christians from loving concern for those persons. "Love your enemies; do good to those who persecute you." Nor is there to be a limit beyond which Christians can feel themselves freed from loving others: "Love one another as I have loved you." Nothing is clearer in the New Testament writings than this commandment of Christian love.

It is evident how such love would alter the lives of those

men and women toward whom it would be directed, to say nothing of the lives of the Christians who loved in this fashion. Human beings develop as persons by relating to one another. Not only do they broaden the horizons of their own experience and consciousness by sharing in the ideas and interests of others, it is in this interchange with others that they discover their own distinctive self-identity. To deprive a human of all love is effectively to deny him the possibility of attaining his own selfhood. There is no greater need or right that a man has than that of friendly association with his fellow-man and there is no greater gift that one person can give another than his gift of self in love.

This is true not just of persons. Like persons, societies can be open or closed. Whether nations or groupings within a nation, societies can be corporately fearful and insecure, and consequently can react to other societies with anger and hostility and suspicion. Neuroses can be shared by groups of men and women, and can find expression in prejudice and militarism and hatred. Such group fear and insecurity is one of the gravest threats to human freedom and peace.

On the other hand, if such societies were dominated by concern for other societies and were trustful of those other societies, it would be incomparably easier to resolve the national and international tensions which at times threaten our very existence. It may seem an unrealizable dream that such an atmosphere of openness and trust, such an attitude of love and concern, could ever come into being. But if it did, it would have immense effect on the practicalities of human life. Christianity's ideal— that such love among men might come into existence through the efforts of Christians (along with others) and the power of Christ's own Spirit of love — may, then, be thought of as almost unattainable, but it cannot be said to be impractical.

4. Since it proposes a distinctive set of values, and since it advocates love as a way of life, Christianity stresses *concern for others as a basic human motivation*. Christ himself is most truly the man for other men. His redemptive action con-

sists in the gift of himself to others, so that these others may experience life more authentically and fully. So, too, the mission of the Christian community is grounded in Christians' concern for their contemporaries. They must be so concerned, but they must also work to spread this concern to the other men and women of their world.

It is not enough for people, or societies, to agree theoretically with a certain set of values. Some strong motivation must be brought into play, so that those values are expressed concretely in men's activity. The search for wealth, the quest for power, the desire for fame and glory: These have proved themselves effective motivations. So have anger and hatred. What Christianity proposes is that true human concern for others become the moving force in human society, so that the values advocated by the Gospel be brought into men's lives.

Here, as in other regards, the viewpoint of the New Testament literature is down-to-earth: it recognizes the presence of selfishness, fear, and lethargy in society; it recognizes that men need redemption from such forms of evil. But, say the New Testament writers, this redemption has occurred. Jesus has completed the saving work of his death and resurrection by sending into the world his own Spirit, and it is the impulse of this Spirit that should move men to be concerned for one another and to build the kind of human society that would make it possible for men and women to live in freedom and justice and dignity.

Strong motivation of this kind is needed if justice is ever to prevail in human society. Justice is hard to define in the concrete circumstances of human life, for it is often difficult to resolve the conflicting interests and rights of individuals or groups. If it is difficult to make the correct judgment about what is just or unjust in a given case, it is even more difficult to implement such a judgment in the face of powerful forces that may be opposed to the suggested settlement. Only if there is, on all sides, a true concern for others, can there be any ultimate righting of the injustices that oppress people.

Once more, Christians can lay no claim to uniqueness in

insisting on such concern for one's fellow-men. One of the hopeful aspects of our own day is the prominence of this motivation in a number of movements that have recently come into being. But Christians are given no alternative if they will seriously espouse the teaching of the New Testament writings. The Gospel parable that describes the final judgment of mankind makes concern for others the basic criterion for deciding the ultimate destiny of men: "I was hungry and you gave me food . . . as you did it to one of the least of these my brethren, you did it to me" (Mt. 25:34-46).

5. Christians are meant, in carrying out their mission, to *transmit the Spirit of Christ* to other men and to other communities of men. They are to share their own joy and hope, which are rooted in the power and presence of the Spirit. They are meant to work for the peace and human unity that are the intended results of the Spirit's activity among men.

To the extent that it could achieve such results in a world that is painfully torn by dissension, the Christian community would be most relevant. Again, however, it may seem unrealistic to talk about the Spirit helping to solve the actual problems of war and strife. Yet one of the greatest barriers to the overcoming of these evils is the discouragement and despair of people, their lack of hope that any solution can be found. To provide such hope is, therefore, a necessary part of the immense task of attacking these evils. By the very fact that they have been entrusted with the Gospel, Christians are deputed to bring hope to their fellow-men. The Gospel is a message of hope, of hope that is grounded in the abiding presence of the risen Lord and of his Spirit.

The New Testament writings do seem to provide the Christian people today with important guidelines for their life in the world, even if these writings do not provide detailed practical suggestions. They could scarcely do the latter, since the early Christian community that produced the New Testament literature was living in a social situation very different from our own.

One must admit that, for the most part, the teaching of the

New Testament is directed at the transformation of individual Christians, or at the deepening of the Christian community's own corporate existence; relatively little attention is paid to the social institutions in which the early Christians found themselves involved. We can notice some probings in this direction, though, as in the latter half of the letter to the Ephesians. After the first half of the letter explains the mystery of Christians' union with the risen Christ, a union so profound that they form "one body" with him, the second portion suggests the attitudes and behavior appropriate to Christians as they participate in various social structures. What is important to our present-day reflection on such passages is not the concrete suggestions made by a New Testament author, but the basic teaching that membership in the body of Christ does have implications for Christians' life in the world. It remains for each generation of Christians to determine more precisely what those implications are in their given set of circumstances. In large part, this is the proper task of the people of God, to which Vatican II's Constitution on the Church points in its chapter on the laity.

One can also gain a certain amount of insight into the impact that Christianity is meant to have on man's social institutions, if one recalls that the Church's mission is a sharing in Christ's own messianic mission. This mission, in the view of the New Testament theologians, is the fulfillment of Old Testament texts such as Isaiah 11 (which we examined earlier). Such passages see the messianic achievement as one of restructuring society, so that justice and peace and true community result.

The Role of the Institution

At this point in the discussion, however, we encounter a crucial question. Even if one grants that Christian faith and commitment, as described for us in the New Testament documents, demand an involvement of Christians in the world of their day and specifically in the reconstruction of social institutions, does it follow that the Church itself is to be institutionally involved? Should the Church as an organized and structured social reality become engaged in the secular sphere? Or is it not sufficient, indeed preferable, that the social impact of Christianity come through the dedicated efforts of Christian men and women who are actively engaged in the social and political life of their day?

There are no easy or obvious answers to these questions. They touch the very heart of the Catholic Church's present reappraisal of its role in history and it's "rediscovery" of the role of the lay men and women in the Church. As civil society assumes more responsibility for the aged, the indigent, and others needing care, there is no longer the need that existed earlier for concerned groups, such as the Church, to fill in this gap. Christians, for the reasons we have been describing, should be active participants in these "secular" efforts to remedy social ills and build a better life for all men; and it is very likely that they will be more effective if they do not act through formal Church agencies.

On the other hand, there seems to be no good reason why a group of people, in order to be more productive in their activity, should not decide to act corporately. It would seem logical that groups of Christians, interested in creating the kind of society that fosters human freedom and security and happiness, would band together by themselves or with others and work for needed changes in society. What seems to be critical in all such endeavors — and to this the Constitution on the Church in the Modern World of Vatican II points — is that they be directed outward to the needs of men and not be dominated by a group's own internal needs.

One thing has become increasingly clear during the past century: The Church as an institutional reality is not meant to be a political or economic power alongside the nations of the world. The power the Church is meant to exercise lies in the moral and religious sphere, and the leaders of the Church should be able to proclaim publicly the moral persuasion of the Christian people on important social issues. Because of a backlog of historical experience in which Church leaders, particularly the Pope, functioned as civil rulers (for example, the centuries during which the pope as sovereign of the papal states actually governed a civil state), the Catholic Church has not yet completely freed herself of a "realpolitik" mentality. An evolution, is going on, however, in which the authority structure of the Church is gradually abandoning a political use of power in favor of the kind of influence that is appropriate to the Gospel.

Much of this "new" manner of thinking was crystallized at the Second Vatican Council. Even though the most important document of the Council was its Constitution on the Church, the Council was characterized by its shift of emphasis from the Church herself to the mystery of Christ. In marked contrast to Vatican I, Vatican II was Christ-centered in its mentality. To the extent that it laid stress on the function of Christ and his Spirit in the life of the Church, the Council necessarily deemphasized the ecclesiastical structures of the Christian community and emphasized its inner dynamism.

In the last analysis, what this means is that the relevance of the Church in the contemporary world is the relevance of the risen Christ himself. While the members of the Church are able to contribute to the betterment of mankind their human dedication, their professional competence in various fields of knowledge and action, their time and energy, these are things that can be given by any idealistic and generous person. The only unique contribution that Christianity can make to the development of mankind is Christ himself — a contribution which, if the faith of Christians be true, is a most decisive one.

According to the worldview of Christian faith, man has been given by God the charge of building his world. The course of history is left to the freedom of man, which God respects. On the other hand, man is incapable by his own unaided efforts of achieving a world order that would be appropriate to men. Mankind is touched, and to some extent debilitated, by the influence of evil; men need redemption not just to reach some otherworldly goal ("heaven"), but even to make of this world a fit situation for human life. Jesus of Nazareth, having passed through death into the role of the risen Lord, is the savior of men. He is, then, enduringly relevant to human history. Derivatively, the Christian community which makes him effectively present to men is enduringly relevant.

Christianity's relevance is, accordingly, directly proportionate to the extent to which it can make the presence of Christ effective in the lives of men. While the prophetic function of the Church, her preaching of the Gospel, may at first sight seem to be out of touch with the pressing problems of our contemporary world, it is, according to the faith of the New Testament community and of the Church today, the source of mankind's contact with its savior, the risen Christ.

CHAPTER THREE

The Changing Church

FOR MANY CATHOLICS the Second Vatican Council was a source of hope and rejoicing; for many others it was and has continued to be a source of alarm. The reason is the same for each reaction: The Council initiated change in many aspects of Catholic thought and life, and it gave promise of yet greater change to come. To many, Catholic and non-Catholic alike, the Roman Catholic Church had given the appearance of an institution that was solidly entrenched in patterns of creed and ritual and hierarchy, safely beyond any influence that would challenge the unchangeableness of its faith or life. With Vatican II, that image of the monolithic and immutable Church was shattered. The ensuing period has been one of deep unrest for many members of the Church.

Vatican II, however, did not modify the nature of the Church. It did bring to clearer light the deeper vitality of the Church, the currents of growth and development that witness to the Spirit's constant activity in the Church. To those who were aware of the immense and radical changes taking place in modern society, who saw the possible threat in such change to the dignity and rights of human beings throughout the world, this "new view" of the Church (which, as we will see, is not all that new) gave promise of Christianity's ability to share in the task of building a future appropriate to man. The Church, which many had written off as archaic and irrelevant, seems now quite capable of moving with the times and even able to provide much-needed leadership.

Change and Tradition

Change, however, always involves risk. What is taking place in our contemporary world may result in unprecedented freedom and security for men and women of all levels of society or it may result in new forms of oppression and enslavement. Many have watched the developments of our day with considerable trepidation, fearing that much of a cultural heritage won with great effort will be quickly dissipated. To such people the changes occurring in the Catholic Church are particularly threatening, since the Church had seemed to be a symbol of stability, tradition, and adherence to unchanging truth.

Such expectations of the Church as the guardian of tradition are well-grounded. Tradition is especially important in the Church's existence. Secular society would be greatly impoverished, were it to lose its cultural and social traditions; were the Church to lose her tradition, she would pass out of existence. It is through tradition that the object of Christian faith is transmitted from one generation to another. Without this object of faith, a faith-community would have no principle of unity or source of life.

Safeguarding tradition does not, however, require resistance to development and change. The movements in Catholic thought and life that underlie much of the current ferment in the Church (Scripture studies, liturgical revival, catechetical renewal) have been in large part a "return to the sources," a search for the most basic and controlling traditions of the Christian heritage. What has become more apparent is that the retention of those living insights and personal relationships upon which the Christian community draws for its life requires organic growth and alteration of the external forms in which these insights and relationships are expressed.

Faced with the inevitability and desirability of such organic change, the Catholic Church (as well as other Christian Churches) is trying to ascertain more clearly the criteria by which she can evaluate the various elements of change, so that the discontinuity intrinsic to it does not destroy the continuity of faith and life upon which the Church's very existence depends.

Difficult though it may be to face, alteration of external structure is not the heart of the matter. For example, were it to prove practically desirable, the entire structure of cardinals and curial congregations could vanish without endangering any essential aspect of the Church's life or teaching. What does touch at the very heart of Christian tradition, and therefore at the essential identity of the Church throughout the course of history, is the modern world's stress on the relativity of truth.

Is there such a reality as "absolute truth"? For the most part the contemporary intellectual world would give a negative answer to this question. The relativity of knowledge, even in the fields of physical science, and the increased awareness of the subjective dimension in all human knowing seem to support this negative response. Where such a denial of absolute truth touches men most threateningly is in the area of ethical judgment. Without some ultimate truth as a touchstone for evaluating human actions as ethically good or bad, how can human society hope to endure? Without some ultimate criteria of judgment, human behavior can be guided only by expediency.

There can be no honest denial of the extent to which human knowledge is subjective and relative. To reject the valid evidence that modern scholarship has amassed in this regard would be itself a rejection of truth. Christianity could not legitimately deny this evidence, nor need it do so. The opposition between modern emphasis on the relativity of human knowing and the Church's emphasis on dogma is not as total as it may seem.

The Church herself has become more aware in recent decades that the definition of dogmas, i.e. the statement of certain religious truths as "irreformable," must itself be seen as part of the Church's evolving life of faith. The notion that dogma could develop, a notion that was regarded as dangerous when Newman spoke of it in the middle of the nineteenth century, is today accepted by Catholic scholars as commonplace. This does not mean, however, that there is agreement among such scholars as to the nature or the extent of such development.

What faces us in the Church today is the unavoidable task of putting together into a consistent understanding the elements of "sameness" and "difference" as they touch religious belief. This is much more than assembling together the pieces of knowledge that have remained unchanged and those that have changed. Both continuity and discontinuity of understanding have touched all the central mysteries of Christian faith: Trinity, Incarnation, Eucharist, and others. In its historical existence, the Church has lived her faith, and like everything alive, this faith retained its radical sameness in the midst of vital development.

Change and the Scriptures

The experience of the biblical communities, Old Testament Israel and early Christianity, as we find it reflected in the text of Scripture, is a profitable guide for the Church today as she faces the questions we have been discussing. Here, as in so many other matters, we can notice the parallel between our own situation and that of the men who produced the biblical literature. Without being able to find any ready-made solutions, we can discover certain guidelines and basic attitudes.

One conclusion certainly should emerge from a study of the Bible: Change is not something to fear. On the contrary, Scripture shows that the moments of greatest change in the life of Israel or of early Christianity were the moments of greatest revelation. They were also, by the very force of events, the moments of most radical conversion and spiritual development. This is not to say that such "crises" were without pain and uncertainty; they generally involved a great deal of both. But they proved to be the focal points around which the process of "salvation history" unfolded.

In many respects, the Exodus was the paradigmatic experience by which both Israel and early Christianity understood their life of faith. The traditions of the Exodus and of the sojourn of the people in the desert present an ideal of religious behavior to which the prophets and other religious leaders could appeal. The Exodus was, of course, the period of constant change, the period when practically no structured forms existed to guide the people's life and faith. It was during this time when Israel was "on the move" that Yahweh was nearest to her and she most open to him.

When we ask why this should be, a number of reasons suggest themselves. Because of the newness and uncertainty of the situation, it was necessary for the people to live in expectancy. They had to listen to the dictates of the new experience; they had to learn from it in order to preserve their individual and social existence. Such an attitude conditioned them for a "new look" at God, prepared them for the openness of faith that was needed if revelation was to be given them.

In contrast, the settled and sedentary life which the people enjoyed after their conquest of the land and the establishment of the kingdoms was much more of a threat to the integrity of Israel's faith. Relatively prosperous and organized, with an established liturgy apparently safeguarding the continuance of religion and a "divinely-established" kingship promising unending earthly security, the people's consciousness of Yahweh and sense of dependence on him was dimmed. It took the painful and unsettling experience of exile to shake the people — or at least a remnant of them — from their unjustified complacency and lead them back to their heritage of faith.

This is not to glorify mobility and change for its own sake. The Old Testament traditions do present as an ideal the "promised land," a place where Israel can dwell in peace and tranquillity. Still, mobility was not a barrier to religious growth. The early Christians seem to have consciously grasped this lesson. They ascribe their own wanderings and relatively unsettled life to the impetus of the Spirit. They propose detachment from settled abode and accumulated possessions as an ideal for one who would effectively preach the Gospel. Jesus himself "had not whereon to lay his head."

There seems no doubt — though the evidence on this point must be gained from a historical period later than that represented by the New Testament writings — that a settled and favorable social situation has not always proved a benefit to the Church. To a large extent, the Church, like Israel before her, has found her greatest spiritual growth in the times of adversity. These occasions, which seemed to forbode grave threat to the Church's life, proved to be the "moments of truth" when the Christian community rediscovered itself as a community of faith and the Spirit, and drew from that faith and that Spirit in order to survive.

As it is presented to us in the New Testament writings, the Church's openness to modes of thought other than those she already possessed, to new patterns of community life dictated by new social contexts, even to varying emphases in the proclamation and explanation of the Gospel, is intrinsic to her nature as a missionary community. The Christian community's own existence is for the sake of the Gospel, so that the good news of Christ's resurrection can be shared with all men. This purpose of evangelization dictates the forms of the community's life and activity. Without failing to preach with integrity the one Gospel of Jesus Christ, the Church must adapt herself to the cultural milieu of the people to whom the Gospel is preached.

Rooted in the Jewish culture and experience of Jesus and his early disciples, primitive Christianity had to adjust the categories of thought and the way of life drawn from that context and fit them to a mode of understanding and pattern of life appropriate to the Greco-Roman world. That this was not completely easy is shown by the "conflict of doctrine" between Paul and Peter regarding the manner in which Gentile converts were to be treated. That the adaptation was achieved to a remarkable extent within a few decades is attested to by the fact that the catechesis of the early Church is preserved for us in the Greek language.

Change and the Christian Community

The more one reflects on the short period of time that is represented by the New Testament writings, the more one realizes the remarkable and rapid change that characterized those decades. Much of this development was due, of course, to the fact that the early Christians were only beginning to discover their identity as a community and their role in continuing Christ's redemptive work. It was also due to the fact that events very quickly pushed the Christians out of a settled situation in Jerusalem and forced them to disperse to other cities of the ancient Mediterranean world. The early Christians themselves attributed their missionary restlessness to the impetus of the Spirit, primarily. It was the impulse of the Spirit that directed them to new cities and countries, that opened up to them new modes of life and activity, that inspired them when they faced audiences whose mentalities they did not that thoroughly grasp.

Early Christianity was not, at least for the most part, worried about being new. The letters of Paul, in fact, indicate that the early Christians emphasized the newness of the Gospel they preached. They came to give Jew and Gentile alike a hope they had never had before. They proposed to both a new way of life, a new law. At least implicitly, they looked upon themselves as agents of change; they preached to people the need for the radical personal change that is conversion to Christ.

It would be an error, though, to suppose that early Christianity was naive about the matter of continuity and discontinuity in religious tradition. The fact that we possess the New Testament Scriptures is a clear indication that the Christians of those early decades saw the need of preserving the apostolic catechesis as a guide in preserving unity of faith. Besides, that catechesis itself is profoundly affected by the question of Christianity's continuity or discontinuity with the traditions of Old Testament Israel.

For the early Church, a radically new principle of continuity for the community's faith and life had become available: the presence to the community of the risen Christ and his Spirit. It was in their faith-contact with Christ than the individual Christians found their own identity as believers and their Christian identification with one another. Christ himself functioned as the basic principle of community, rather than teachings or structures or ritual. These latter did serve as sources of unity, but their effectiveness was dependent upon the more basic influence of Christ's presence.

But this very presence of Christ, which provided for their unity and social stability, was the stimulus to constant change. Christ was then, as he is for Christianity today, the most powerful force of discontinuity with past achievements or with tradition. Christ is always a challenge to Christians, individually or in community, demanding a fullness of commitment and faith that they have not yet reached. Contact with him is always a call to conversion. This is the underlying theme of all the moral exhortation of the Pauline epistles.

Because of the risen Christ, the Christian community exists eschatologically. As an imperfect and partial reflection of the redeeming power of Christ who abides with it, the Church is always striving toward a fuller realization of its being and its mission. It is essentially and dynamically oriented toward the future. At the same time, precisely because of the presence of Christ and of his Spirit, the Church already possesses the reality from which she springs and toward which she grows. She is a living "recollection" of Christ's saving death and resurrection, a living "promise" of the final achievement of human history.

As such, the Church is a community of hope. She lives in hope and conveys this hope to men of every historical period. It is in moments of history when change is greatest that this hope is most needed, because the risks are greater at such times. If hope does prevail — and to have it prevail is part of the Church's mission — these are also moments of creativity and advance.

Making the concrete prudential judgments that are involved in social change is always a delicate task. Both a lethargic or frightened clinging to old patterns and a precipitous jettisoning of tradition must be avoided. History is a valuable guide in making such decisions, for mankind has always faced these crises, and our present generation can learn from both the successes and failures of the past. More precisely, the religious experience of Israel and early Christianity, as it is recorded for us in the biblical writings, is a valuable guide for the decisions the Church faces today.

Lessons from History

Two instances immediately come to mind of parallels to our present situation of drastic social and religious change: the reaction of Judaism to Hellenistic culture around the time of the Maccabean revolt, and the conflict over Judaizing tendencies within the infant Church. Both offer valuable insights into the dynamics that are operative in such crisis-situations. Both display the kind of balanced judgment that such crises demand.

Palestinian Judaism's encounter with Hellenistic culture was prepared for by the military conquests of Alexander the Great, during the decade 340-330 B.C. Moving invincibly through the Near East, he shattered the power of Egypt and Persia and extended his empire as far east as India. Before dying at an early age, he divided his conquests among his generals, thus bringing into being the Hellenistic kingdoms that were dominant in the Near East until the ascendancy of the Romans. Of special importance to the last few centuries of Old Testament history were the Seleucid kingdom, with its capital at Antioch in Syria, and the Ptolemaic kingdom, with its center at Alexandria in Egypt.

Until about 200 B.C. the Jews in Palestine were under the rule of the Ptolemies, who permitted the Jews a considerable amount of freedom and self-determination. At the beginning of the second century B.C. the Seleucid rulers moved against Egypt and in the course of this military venture brought the Jews under their sovereignty. As part of their domination,

they set about imposing Hellenistic culture on the Jewish
populace. This policy of cultural imperialism reached a high
point during the reign of Antiochus Epiphanes IV (175-
163). Jewish religious practice was proscribed, a Hellenistic
cult was forced on the people, and the Jerusalem Temple itself was desecrated in 167 (1 Mac. 1).

As the oppression of the Seleucids became intolerable and
the religious heritage of Israel was threatened with destruction, the family of the Maccabees, in 164 B.C., led the Jews
in a revolt which resulted in the overthrow of Syrian domination and the reestablishment of Jewish worship in the Temple. (1 Mac. 2-4) For about a century, the Jews enjoyed relative autonomy and freedom, both in politics and in religion.

During this period, which was one of deep cultural change
in the entire Near East, the reaction of Jews to the process
of Hellenization was mixed. Even the books of Maccabees,
which glorify the "traditionalist" reaction against Hellenism,
admit the tendency of many Jews to embrace the "modern"
thought and life of Greece. Some Jews went so far as to
adopt Greek names; they abandoned the ancient practice of
circumcision that had served as a mark of their Jewish religious identity; they participated in the Greek games and cultural events, events which probably had religious overtones.
Though the Maccabean revolt and the ensuing religio-politi-
cal situation of the Jews in Palestine represented the triumph
of the anti-Hellenization forces, the impact of Hellenistic culture continued to be felt in Jewish life and thought, particularly among the wealthy and the aristocracy.

In this period of tension and conflict, one can see some of
the problems that any religious community will face in a situation of major cultural change. On the one side, the enthusiastic and uncritical adoption of Hellenistic thought and
social institutions threatened the cherished traditions of Old
Testament Israel and the continued existence of the Jews as a
distinctive social force. On the other side, the opposition to
Hellenistic "modernism" — which in the case of some groups
bordered on fanaticism — brought with it a rigid adherence

to established religious forms, a narrow chauvinism, and a cultural isolationism that threatened the internal development of Judaism itself.

Perhaps the gravest danger in Judaism's confrontation with Hellenization was that of factionalism, the division of Jews into opposing sects whose bitter conflicts destroyed the community of the Jewish people. During the two centuries prior to the Christian era and right up to the Roman destruction of Jerusalem in 70 A.D., this sectarian controversy kept the Jews at constant odds with one another and prevented them from attaining unity even in the face of national extinction.

The second historical instance that is instructive for us is early Christianity's struggle to relate itself to, and yet distinguish itself from, Judaism. Although unquestionably affected by the Judaism-Hellenism controversy we have just examined, the tension in the early Church between her own "newness" and her Old Testament roots was quite different. Rather than a conflict between religion and "secular" culture, it was a conflict between established religious institutions and categories (Judaism) and new religious ideas and forms. Moreover, the proponents of Christianity's radical newness based their case, not on the need to be up-to-date and in tune with the "modern world," but on a new and more ultimate revelation.

The problem was this: Many of the early converts from Judaism to Christianity, while they accepted the risen Christ as the Messiah and the fulfillment of Judaism, wished to retain within Christianity the distinctive practices of Judaism. This came down to the insistence that the Old Testament laws must remain in force for Christians. Not only did these "Judaizers" wish to claim for themselves the right to preserve their Jewish traditions, they attempted to impose these traditions on the entire Christian community, even on the converts from the Gentile world.

Paul's letters are an important witness to the depth of this controversy, for Paul was the leading opponent of this Judaizing tendency. He saw that this movement, if successful, would

reduce Christianity to a sect of Judaism and would close off
the hope of evangelizing the Gentile peoples — his own Spir-
it-inspired mission. As a result, he undertook an outspoken
campaign against the Judaizing threat and forced a thorough
examination of the manner in which Christianity was related
to Old Testament Israel. Humanly speaking, it was largely
through Paul's efforts that early Christianity was able to claim
the right to find its own identity and its own destiny.

No New Testament passage speaks more poignantly of the
human tensions involved in this situation than Galatians 2-3.
Here, Paul describes the occasion of his confrontation with
Peter. The latter, though personally in agreement with Paul's
approach to Gentile converts, had allowed the Judaizing fac-
tion to exert undue influence on him. For this, Paul blames
him, and insists that salvation comes from faith in the risen
Christ rather than from the old law. Apparently, the frank
words of Paul were effective. At any rate, the independence
of Christianity from restrictive elements of Judaism was
clearly established well before the end of the apostolic era.

On the other hand, the letters of Paul and the Gospels both
stress the deep continuity of Christian faith and life with the
sacred traditions of Israel. So true is this that it would be impossible to grasp the meaning of the New Testament writings
if one were entirely without knowledge of the Old Testament
literature. In the view of the early Christians, God's dealings
with Israel and with the Church form one unified and pro-
gressing process of salvation history. Israel is the stage of
promise and preparation, Christianity the stage of fulfillment.

Again, reflection on this early Christian crisis of continuity
and change tells us much about the dynamics of our present-
day moment of decision. The impetus to change in the
Church today does not come alone from the need to make
Christianity relevant to the evolving patterns of contemporary
culture. Fundamentally, it comes from within Christianity itself, from the challenge its own internal "newness" always
provides. Christian faith must express itself in some institutional forms; it must necessarily become an "established reli-

gion." Yet, no form that it takes can possibly exhaust Christianity's inner dynamism. This inner vitality is always "new wine" that cannot be contained within "old wine-skins."

While the Church today does not face the precise question of moving from Judaism into the Gentile world, she faces the need to bring the Gospel to cultural contexts she has not yet touched. In these, too, Christianity is meant to find expression, so that the catholicity of the Church can be realized. This missionary effort, like that of Paul to the Gentiles, may not be allowed to be strangled by narrow adherence to established forms. At the same time, in its willingness to speak to this cultural pluralism, the Christian community must continue to speak the one and only Gospel of the risen Christ.

What history teaches us is that times of great change demand an open mind and balanced judgment. Simplistic adherence to extreme positions generally creates more heat than light. The humble search for a more nuanced position is less dramatic, but usually results in a more honest estimate of the realities of the situation and contributes more to a genuine solution. There is certainly need for Christians in such moments to speak their convictions fearlessly; the example of Paul with Peter is unmistakable. These convictions, however, should be spoken as Paul's were: in the spirit of true community, which permits a straightforward interchange in an atmosphere of faith and love.

Such, then, are some of the basic attitudes towards change that one can gain from examination of the religious experience of Israel and early Christianity. What is left is the more extensive task of delineating the exact areas of change and projecting a course of action for each of these areas. Again careful study of the biblical writings is critical. If Christian faith is true, neither the full dimension of the questions nor the full context for their solutions can be known apart from faith and from the guidance given faith by Scripture.

There are many possible ways of classifying the various aspects of Christianity's continuity and discontinuity. A handy scheme is provided by sociologists of religion, who divide religious phenomena into *creed, cult,* and *community;* some add *code* as a fourth element, others include it under creed. While this division does have its inadequacies, it can serve as a structure for our discussion. Within each of these areas there is a continuity/discontinuity tension. While the ultimate principles for understanding and utilizing these tensions creatively apply to all three, the specific application to each area requires clarification.

Creed

Religions necessarily develop a creed, that is, an agreed-upon verbal formulation of the religious insights of the community. Without such a credal formulation, it would be impossible to identify those who share a common faith. Faith and creed are not, however, identical. Creed serves to clarify faith by giving it expression. It also serves to form faith as members are progressively initiated into the community, and it serves as an instrument by which those in the community can discover the basic identity of their faith. Faith itself is broader and more fundamental. Authentic religious faith always transcends creed, and for that very reason demands that creed not remain static.

When we study the question of continuity/discontinuity as it touches the credal statements of Christianity, we are dealing with what is widely referred to as "the development of dogma." Until recently it was considered dangerous, even incorrect, to speak of dogma "developing," at least in Roman Catholic theology. A certain rigidity had crept into the manner of thinking about the "irreformability" of dogmatic statements, as if the formulation of a dogmatic statement froze the understanding of a given mystery into an absolutely unchangeable category.

From one point of view it is difficult to understand how this rigid position came to be prevalent, since at least twice before in history the Roman Church had fought for the principle of credal growth: at the time of the dispute with Eastern Orthodoxy, which wished to limit such growth to the early

Councils of the Church; and at the time of the Reformation when the more radical currents of Protestant thought tended to refuse any reformulation after the Bible.

From another point of view, the fear and hesitancy caused by the notion of dogmatic evolution is understandable. The fact that the Church has solemnly formulated statements about elements of Christian faith and proposed these as sure guides for the orthodoxy of faith and worship, implies that there is some absolute and unchanging truth which these formulations, i.e. dogmas, are expressing. To suggest that these dogmas themselves do, and must, evolve seems to threaten the very notion of absolute truth, as well as the historical unity of Christian faith.

One can, of course, give a response to this problem by drawing a distinction between truth itself and man's possession of it. Truth itself may be absolute, but man's grasp of this truth is always inadequate and relative. However, this "solution" does not suffice, especially when there is question of the truths involved in Christian faith. Christians believe that this faith is grounded in God's revelation; it is inconceivable that God should at any point contradict a truth he has earlier revealed. In some fashion or other, the truth that God has revealed must remain unchanged.

When we turn to the New Testament literature for some guidance in this matter, we can profitably examine the early Church's understanding of faith as "life." Although there is no technical analysis of Christian faith as life by the New Testament writers, they indicate that there is an intrinsic link between the two realities. Often, when Jesus' action of healing is described in the Gospels, this restoration of bodily life and health is associated with faith. After healing someone, Jesus says "Your faith has made you whole." Or it is stated that he could work no wonders of healing in a certain place, because the people did not have faith in him (Mk. 6:5).

The life that is connected with faith is, essentially, something that deals with the higher levels of man's existence —

with his consciousness and decision-making ability. Faith is a receptivity to the word of God, but this word is itself a life-giving and life-preserving word. The Old Testament literature already speaks in these terms of the word of God. What the New Testament adds is the belief that this word of life is the risen Christ, the incarnate Word.

Faith, is, then, a critical component of Christian living. It is a vital activity without which a person would be cut off from the very source of life. It is life in the fullest sense, life in the Spirit which opens onto everlasting life in union with the risen Christ. Christian faith, acceptance of Christ who is the word of life, is the basic thing required of a man if he wishes to live. "This is the work of God, that you believe in him whom he has sent" (Jn. 6:29).

If faith is an element of life, it must grow and develop. This is a basic law of all created life. Life demands continuing change; when a living being is completely static it is no longer alive. This is true of human beings, not only with respect to their biological life, but also with respect to their intellectual and affective life. Unfortunately, many men and women are "dead" on this personal level of their life long before bodily death occurs. And from history we see that the same thing occurs in social groups like organizations or nations or religions.

New Testament writers reflect the early Christian community's understanding that faith is meant to grow and develop into maturity. This understanding can be expressed in a parable like that of the man who went out to plant seed in the ground, or in Paul's exhortation to cherish and nourish the gift of life that has come with the Gospel; but the message is essentially the same. God's work in the lives of the early Christians had begun in a new way with their exposure to the good news of the risen Christ, but this work must be brought to fulfillment. New life had begun, but it had not yet reached maturity.

If the personal level of human life (including faith) is to grow, the person must be exposed to new experiences, to new ideas, to new people, so that in response to them he can expand the range of his interests and of his awareness. This is true also of nations or of religious communities. Unless they come into contact with other groups and are forced to interact with them, they stagnate and eventually die.

The early decades of Christianity are a striking instance of the rich growth in self-awareness that can come to a group if it is forced to contact different cultural or religious influences. Moving as quickly as it did throughout the ancient Mediterranean basin, the infant Church encountered a wide variety of religious beliefs, philosophical ideas, and social structures. Out of this came different ways of understanding and explaining Christianity, even a certain diversity of traditions about the words and deeds of Jesus, as the four versions of the Gospel indicate. Without losing touch with the saving event of Christ's death and resurrection, the early Christian communities developed rapidly in their understanding and formulation of the Gospel, and did so under the impact of the life-situations into which they moved.

Early Christianity's situation was, of course, unique. This was the period of initial self-identity, the period of establishing forms and structures for the first time, the period when everything was, in a sense, new. The same conditions, however, are true of every historical period, and much of it is true of periods of major cultural change. Changing historical experience always challenges a people's self-understanding and self-expression. As new patterns of life and behavior, new mores and values, emerge, the old ways of doing things and of viewing life no longer fit. Every society goes through such change. Old Testament Israel went through it a number of times; the Church has experienced it repeatedly.

Not all of the decisions made in such periods of change are correct, not all the new "insights" are equally valid. Israel's adjustment to the introduction of kingship into its social and religious existence illustrates this well. Many advantages came with the Davidic rule and with the kingly rule of later monarchs. Israel's social and religious structures were solidified and stabilized, a stronger national identity was forged, a milieu was established in which cultural and religious traditions could more easily develop and find expression.

The kingly ascendancy in Israel's life also brought with it the tendency to depend on political and military solutions as answers to life's most basic problems, and this was an obvious challenge to the primacy of faith. Increased economic prosperity was a blessing, but apparently it was not secured without some exploitation of the poorer classes of Israelitic society.

Though the experience of Babylonian exile and the need to adjust to a shattering change of social structure must have been most painful, the period of exile was one of the most spiritually mature in the history of Israel. No doubt the highly developed culture of Babylon must have been a temptation for many of the deportees, but it also served as a challenge to Israel's own religious insights. It is from this context that we possess the sharply monotheistic passages of Deutero-Isaiah, the "Servant songs" with their deeply spiritual ideal, and some recognition of the universal character of God's covenant providence.

Christianity has not been less influenced by the historical events in which Christians have been involved. Its very claim to be catholic, to fit all cultures and all historical circumstances, lays the Church open to being influenced by all the various evolutions of human thought and social institutions. The supremely revealing event of Jesus' death and resurrection remains always the key source of Christianity's understanding of human life. But as the Christian community moves through history there is a constant acquisition of new knowledge and new experience, which bears in greater or lesser degree on the Church's understanding of her faith.

Because the Church is people, and people are involved in these movements of cultural and social change, there is a constant need for the Church to appraise and modify the manner in which she expresses her own faith. Such reformulation of belief is, admittedly, a delicate matter, for the Church must be careful not to lose the essential message of the Gospel. But this reformulation is unavoidable. The verbal translations of faith that conveyed accurately an understanding of Christ and his redeeming work to one historical period or culture could, if left completely unchanged, convey either no meaning or even a distorted meaning to another historical or cultural situation.

What must be kept in mind is that there are many different ways of understanding and living the mystery of Christ. These can be complementary to one another, each having its own characteristic contribution to make in the process of revealing historically the full implications of Jesus' death and resurrection. These ways need not exclude one another, though the universal Church must always pass judgment on formulations or practices that are basically incompatible with the true understanding of Christianity. Within the limits set by the need to avoid error, a certain pluralism of understanding and social forms should mark the Church's life. This is what has often been referred to in recent centuries as one of the "marks of the Church," its catholicity.

Another of the "marks" of the Church is her unity, particularly her unity of faith. Such unity of belief must apply to the Church not only in the sense that, at a given point in history, there is basic agreement among Christians throughout the world, but also in the sense that a fundamental unity of belief is sustained throughout history. Were the Church today, for example, to lose the basic insights of faith that were possessed and transmitted by the early Christians, she could not justifiably call herself "Christian."

Some permanence and universality in the dogmatic formulations of faith that have come into existence during the past two thousand years are obviously needed. If Christians today share the same faith that Christians had in the first century, or at the time of the Council of Chalcedon, or at the time of the First Vatican Council, then the expression of faith that one finds in the New Testament writings or in the dogmatic decrees of those Councils can still have meaning for present-day Christians. While there is growth and development of understanding, there cannot be essential disagreement among those various professions of faith; were there such, it would indicate that there did not exist a fundamental unity of faith throughout the centuries.

Dogmas and creeds issued by councils do not, of course, have the same privileged role that Scripture itself has, for they are not the "word of God" as the Bible is. They do have a positive, though limited, function as guides and norms of faith. These doctrinal formulations, however, are not the object of Christian faith. Faith is the acceptance of Christ, of his Father, of the Spirit who acts in the Church, of the mystery of redemption; it is these realities towards which faith is directed. Even the most solemn of dogmatic decrees is only a statement about these realities, and it is recognized as true by the believing community because it corresponds to these realities.

Dogmatic decrees or creeds cannot, therefore, be the root principle of the historical continuity of faith. It is the risen Christ himself and his Spirit at work in the Church who play this function of ultimately safeguarding the unity of Christian faith. Christ himself, "the same yesterday, today, and forever," is the one towards whom all authentic Christian faith is directed. He, the one mystery of Christ, is the one whom all creeds and dogmas are trying to describe. While different cultures and different historical periods may look at him from distinct points of view, while they may emphasize different aspects of his saving work, or experience that saving power in quite different contexts of life, they all ultimately converge in him as the one, same, risen Lord.

The New Testament literature itself is a formulation of faith, and like all others is touched by the culture and historical experience of the people who produced it. It has unique value as a unifying source of faith because it is grounded in the primitive Christian experience of the life, death, and resurrection of Jesus. It is this event, to which the New Testament writings bear witness, in which all later generations of Christians believe. It is the meaning of this event that all later credal formulations of Christianity try to express.

Scripture has always been, and must always be, a primary agent of continuity in the Church's life of faith. Later centuries of theological thought or of dogmatic development may (and do) give a more detailed explanation of the mystery of Christ, but what they are explaining is the mystery of which the New Testament books speak. Scripture is the first literary expression of tradition, the organically developing continuity of faith-understanding; it states the tradition of the Church as it existed at the end of the apostolic period. For that reason, it contains at least germinally all that later stages of tradition will state more explicitly. Basic congruence with the New Testament Scriptures is a test of the authenticity of all later formulations of Christian faith.

Cult

Sacraments, too, provide a principle of continuity for Christian faith and life, but they also provide the second major area of change in the Church. For many Catholics this is probably the most noticeable area of alteration in the present-day Church. Accustomed from early years to a liturgy that was absolutely fixed, rubrically controlled, and celebrated in an unknown language, Catholics have seen rapid modifications in little more than a decade. Much of this change has been welcomed by the bulk of people, especially the adoption of vernacular languages instead of Latin, but for some men and women the very notion of such change has been deeply unsettling, and for many others there is a lurking uneasiness about the nature and extent of future changes.

The worry about excessive liturgical change is rooted in a solid Christian instinct. The continuity of faith and tradition is closely linked with sacramental liturgy, particularly with the celebration of the Eucharist, and too drastic a modification of liturgical forms might seriously obscure or endanger faith itself. But a blind resistance to any liturgical flexibility can be equally dangerous. The history of religions seems to indicate that religious ritual goes out of existence or becomes mere superstition if it settles into an absolutely unalterable pattern.

An overly rigid adherence to rubrics — to movements and formulas that are determined in every detail — can easily suggest a mentality of magic. In the rituals of a magical cult, the various words and gestures, their sequence and pattern and number, are considered to have an intrinsic power of their own. If they are performed in exact and proper detail they infallibly bring about a certain desired effect. In such a magical cult there is freedom neither for man nor for the divinity he worships. The divinity is not petitioned, but "forced" to perform a certain act because the ritual action has happened; the devotees are not so much venerating the divinity as they are submitting themselves to the necessary rigmarole in order to obtain what they wish.

Christian liturgy, even in its darkest days, never became this kind of magical ritual. Elements of this mentality did drift into the liturgical attitudes of people and an excessive insistence on liturgical forms as absolutely established did little, if anything, to overcome this tendency. Reverence and grace and dignity, which should characterize any act of worship, are helped by a carefully planned, even somewhat conventionalized, course of actions in liturgy. But such arranged patterns exist only to help liturgy be an authentic expression of Christian gratitude, worship, and devotion.

It may seem odd to raise the question of magic when talking about Christian sacramental actions. Most Catholics would think of magic as something which, if taken as more than a joke, would be found only in some "primitive religions." All religions, nevertheless, including Christianity, have to guard against a magical mentality in their cult. Perhaps it is because men do not believe deeply enough to trust the fidelity of a God with whom they deal in personal relationship, and instead seek a means of securing life and prosperity through some automatically certain means.

Even a cursory reading of the Old Testament literature discloses a constant polemic against magic, especially in the prophetic oracles. Whether the prophets explicitly attack recognized magical practices, or whether they condemn the routinely monotonous performance of Israel's own liturgies, the message is essentially the same: it is vain to expect any results from this pseudo-ritual which wins only "the wrath of God." What Israel should do in its cult is to recall its covenant with Yahweh, a covenant which is ultimately a personal relationship, and pledge itself to fulfilling its own role in this covenant at the same time that it trusts in the fidelity of Yahweh to his covenant promises.

Even early Christianity was not entirely without this problem. In the scene of Jesus' temptation in the desert, the first suggestion made to him by Satan was that he use magical powers: "Change these stones into bread." And Jesus had to warn his followers against an empty and meaningless performance of worship: "If you are offering your gift at the altar, and there remember that your brother has something against you, leave your gift there before the altar and go; first be reconciled to your brother, and then come and offer your gift" (Mt. 5:23-24).

However, the New Testament writings reflect a remarkable and radical shift of attitude towards cult. Compared with the complex liturgical life of Judaism, which would have been familiar to Jesus himself and to his early disciples, the first decades of Christianity seem almost to be without specifically Christian cult. It was not that the Christians were without any cult; rather, the specifically Christian acts of worship were relatively unritualized, were so much a "natural" part of the life-style and activity of the community that they scarcely gave the appearance of liturgy.

This does not mean that there was no form or regularity of pattern in early Christian sacramental practice. While there may well have been more flexibility than we are accustomed to, there is no doubt that a basic similarity marked the initiation of converts through baptism, wherever that occurred in the infant Church. Much the same was true of the community gatherings for the eucharistic "breaking of the bread," to which all the diverse New Testament traditions attest. But nothing suggests the rubrical mentality that dominated the performance of Christian sacraments for many centuries prior to the recent liturgical revival.

What is most important in the New Testament references to early Christian sacramental practice is their understanding of the nature of these acts, for this provides us with an insight into the basic principles of continuity in the Church's liturgical life. Whatever may have been the exact details of the first-century initiation of Christians through baptism, or their celebration of the Eucharist, such actions are inseparably linked with the death and resurrection of Jesus. Not only do they commemorate that new Passover event, they bring Christians into immediate contact with the risen Lord. In baptism the new Christian is joined with, enters into, the death and resurrection of Christ. When Christians gather for Eucharist, they bear witness to Christ's death and glorification, and he himself is there in their midst.

At an early stage (indicated by 1 Cor. 11:23) the notion of "tradition" is already closely connected with the eucharistic celebration. Not only was the community assembly for "the breaking of the bread" a natural occasion for handing on and explaining the apostolic experience of Jesus' life, death, and resurrection, but the very action of Eucharist was the heart of that "handing on," i.e. of the process of tradition. As Paul explains to the Corinthians (1 Cor. 11:26), "as often as you eat this bread and drink the cup, you proclaim the Lord's death until he comes."

Christian sacrament is, then, more than an occasion for explaining the mystery of Christ, more than an opportunity for conveying to a community of believers the traditional understanding of Christ's death and resurrection. It is the making present of this death and resurrection, that is, of the risen Lord himself; it is the handing on (the *tradition,* using this word in an active sense) of the very reality of the mystery of Christ. This is the fundamental aspect of continuity in Christian sacramental liturgy. If the Church lost contact with this tradition, the very nature of Christianity would be radically altered: Instead of being a community that celebrates the presence in its midst of the risen Christ and discovers thereby its own identity as the "body of Christ," the Church would become a community that did nothing more than recall what Jesus had said and done.

In the historical evolution of liturgical forms (an evolution which is inevitable — and beneficial, when properly guided) it is imperative that the Church not lose this central element of her cult, the making present of the mystery of Christ. This means that the basic *significance* of the sacramental actions remains substantially the same, for it is by this significance that sacraments effect the contact of Christians with the risen Christ. Though the external forms of sacramental liturgy may change, in order to speak more effectively to different historical or cultural contexts, they must continue to speak the redeeming presence of the risen Christ.

Thus, the New Testament writings supply us with an insight into the most important principle of liturgical continuity. Christian sacraments contain an extremely rich symbolism (which it is not our purpose to study here); their significance touches all the aspects of meaning in human life. The key symbolism, which characterizes Christian sacraments and distinguishes them from all other religious ritual, is historical: They symbolize and thereby make present the *event* of Christ's death and resurrection.

Old Testament ritual is already a step in the direction of Christian liturgy's emphasis on historical significance. Ritual legislation, like that contained in the book of Leviticus, shows that the great festivals (Passover, Tabernacles, etc.) were commemorative in tone, recalling the "great deeds" of Yahweh on behalf of his people, in particular the events connected with the exodus from Egypt and the entry into the promised land (Ex. 12-13). There is even a suggestion that a past event like the exodus is somehow rendered contemporary to later generations through the agency of liturgy, not in the sense that the actual event itself is made present, but in the sense that the covenant relationship that originated in the past events continues on in the people's life, with each succeeding generation having the opportunity in commemorative liturgy to align itself with this covenant.

Christian celebration of sacraments goes an important step further. As understood by Christian faith, the sacramental actions of the Church not only stand in continuity with Christ's death and resurrection, as did Israelitic ritual with the saving events of Old Testament history, they actually make present the very *event* of Christ's Passover. This is seen as possible because the risen Christ himself is the reality of the resurrection event; he *is* the resurrection. Christian sacraments are, therefore, the preservation of historical tradition in a most unique way. For this reason, they stand at the center of the process of tradition and are an indispensable source of continuity in the Church's faith and life.

At the same time, because they are so essential to the accuracy and growth of faith, it is important that the sacramental actions remain significant for the people who do them. If they are allowed to become unintelligible rituals, sacred acts that men and women perform out of a sense of duty or fear but without understanding, they fail to accomplish the very reason for their existence. Sacraments are of their very nature a "word of revelation" to which the faith of the Christian people is meant to respond. Such a faith-response can be given only if the sacramental actions function adequately as "words."

Sacraments do have what we might call an "objective meaning." The gestures and words that make up a given sacrament — the Eucharist, for example — do themselves signify the presence of the risen Christ, his self-gift to men, the unity of the Christian people. But this objective significance must become operative as meaning, it must convey understanding to the people engaged in the sacramental act.

Christians who participate in a celebration of the Eucharist, or of any other sacrament, must be aware of what this action is saying to them.

To the extent necessary to accomplish this end, and without losing any of the essential meaning, the external forms of liturgical action must fit the lives and understandings of Christians in a given cultural situation or historical period. Obviously, this is a basic reason for the recent shift from Latin to vernacular languages in Catholic sacramental liturgy. For the vast bulk of men and women today the Latin language could no longer function as a means of transmitting meaning; it could not really function as a language. A change of this kind does not by itself accomplish the desired end, but it may be a necessary part of the task of allowing liturgy to speak to people.

This task of forming appropriate sacramental liturgy is delicate and difficult. The symbolisms intrinsic to the sacramental actions are meant to touch, challenge, and transform all the basic symbols and ideas and attitudes that operate in the consciousness and lives of Christians. For this to happen, each action of a sacrament must bear upon the actual life-experience and awareness of the people who are involved in that action. The concrete realities of life must be brought into confrontation with the mystery of Christ's death and resurrection, so that the practical implications of the mystery of Christ can be seen in those realities. This is precisely how men are to become more deeply Christian.

Community

When we turn to the third element of Christianity as a religion, its organized social structures, we touch upon something that may allow much more drastic change than either creed or cult. In the course of the past twenty centuries, the external forms of Christianity as an institutionalized religious community have been altered dramatically from time to time and place to place. The pattern of Christian community life in third-century northern Africa (at the time of St. Cyprian) was certainly different from the monastically-dominated situation of seventh-century Ireland; and both differed considerably from the Catholic Church in the latter half of the nineteenth century.

That there was some measure of continuity in all this is obvious, for historians of the Church can detail much of the process by which any given stage of the historical developments of Church structures was connected with and grew out of what had preceded it. However, this is simply the continuity of one thing succeeding another in time; it does not require that throughout this temporal succession some elements of intrinsic sameness remain. Just as, for example, in a study of the history of governmental structures in Germany in the present century, there would be an obvious level of continuity through the reign of the Kaiser, the structures of the Weimar Republic, the Nazi rule, and the present governmental forms of the West German Republic, it would be impossible to indicate in this series of changes a fundamental identity of governmental structure.

The question, then, as we look at Christianity and examine the continuity of its external social structures is this: Has there been, and must there be, an intrinsic element (or elements) of sameness in the Church's institutional structures? If the answer to this question is affirmative, another immediately follows: What is this necessary element or elements?

It is impossible to obtain a clear response to these questions from the New Testament writings. This is not surprising, since these writings reflect that period of the Church's existence when her external institutions were only coming into being. What the New Testament literature may give us is an insight into the intrinsic nature of the Christian community, of its activity and of its purpose, and therefore some understanding of the structures that are necessary to the Church's existence. This the New Testament does, as we have already seen; its books make clear that the Church is a community of those who believe in the resurrection of Christ, that her purpose is to carry on the redeeming work of the risen Christ, that her activity consists essentially in the proclamation of the Gospel and in the eucharistic worship of the Father.

The touchstone for the essential historical continuity of Christianity is the Christian community's unbroken contact with the event of Jesus' death and resurrection. As long as the risen Christ and his Spirit remain present to this community which accepts the reality of the risen Lord in faith, the continuity of the Church is safeguarded. If the Gospel is preserved and proclaimed from one generation to the next, if its enduring reality is authentically celebrated in sacramental liturgy, Christ himself remains with those who gather together in his name — "even to the end of the world."

Scripture and sacrament function to preserve this continuing identity of faith, but something more is needed. Within the structures of the community's social being, there must be some agency to care for the genuine proclamation of the Gospel and the genuine celebration of sacrament. The Bible by itself cannot prevent its misinterpretation; the sacraments by themselves cannot prevent their erroneous and inadequate performance. The Spirit of Christ works in the Church to prevent such distortions, but the Spirit manifests such guidance through men.

What the New Testament writings point to, and what the immediate post-biblical writings (like the letters of Ignatius of Antioch) state even more clearly, is the existence and need of a group within the community which is charged with safeguarding the tradition contained in Scripture and sacrament. This group has the responsibility, and therefore the authority (for the two must be correlative), of ministering to the Church's unity in faith by proclamation of the word and celebration of the sacraments.

Historically, the group that has laid claim to this special ministry within the Church's life is the episcopal college, the bishops who guide and govern the various communities of Christians throughout the world. While others — priests and deacons, in particular — were associated with them as the task of ministry became more complicated and extensive, it has been (and still is) the episcopal college that essentially constituted this ministerial group. Roman Catholics (and some other Christian Churches as well) believe that such a special ministry within the Church's life is an indispensable element of ecclesial life, and that its existence and function stand in continuity with the role played by the Apostles in the infant Church.

But even if one does accept the permanent need of this special ministry, it would be an oversimplified view of the early Christian evidence and a naive understanding of the way things actually happen in the Church today, if one were to give to the bishops alone the responsibility and the authority for safeguarding faith and worship. The Christian people as a whole is charged with the task of preaching the Gospel and celebrating the sacraments, and different groups within the community — teachers, theologians, those with particular gifts of prayer and insight — have special roles to play in transmitting, clarifying, and nurturing the faith-life of the Church. There is, nevertheless, a specialized task of forming the Christian people into a genuine *community* of faith and worship; this is the task of the episcopacy.

When we ask what this special role is, the most adequate answer seems to be: The episcopal college (and by extension, the other ministers, priests, and deacons, whom the bishops associate with them in their role) is meant to function within the community as a sacrament of the Church's unity of faith and worship. This is the sacrament of orders. As a sacrament, this group is to be a *sign*: a sign of the presence of Christ to the community; a sign of the community's common faith, both at present and in continuity with previous generations of Christians; a sign of the Church's unity in worship; a sign of the Church's corporate dedication to the task of bettering human life. As a sacrament, the episcopal college is to be an *effective* sign, an agency to bring into being the realities it signifies.

What this means concretely is that the bishops fulfill their function both by what they are and by what they do — and it might be good to stress, as Vatican II did, that they fulfill this function corporately. The episcopal college is itself a community of believers, and their corporate profession of faith in the death and resurrection of Jesus of Nazareth is a guide and criterion for the faith of the entire people. They are meant to continue the role of witness that was performed by the Apostles in the infant Church; they thus unify the faith of the Church. However, they are not to form a community of faith simply by their own witness. They are charged with bringing to the Christians of each generation the witness of the Apostles themselves, the witness that is contained in the New Testament writings. They must feed the faith of the Christian people with the Scriptures.

This function is inseparably linked with the bishop's role in the Eucharist. He does not celebrate the Eucharist by himself; the Eucharist is the action of the entire Christian assembly. But the bishop (or the priest who has been delegated as the bishop's "extension"), when he acts as celebrant in the Eucharist, is meant to unify the action. He prays as the representative of the community; it is his prayer that brings into a unified expression the faith of the community. He proclaims and explains the word of God, which intensifies the common understanding and faith of the people and prepares them for a more intense communion in the eucharistic act. Moreover, from the early centuries of the Church onward, the celebrant of the Eucharist has been regarded as a symbol of Christ's own presence to the assembled community, as implementing Christ's act of giving himself to the people under the form of bread and wine.

Since whatever common life-forms Christians adopt, or whatever common apostolic activity they undertake, should be the expression of their response to word and sacrament, the episcopal college acts as a unifying principle for Christian life and action precisely by ministering to the people in word and sacrament. Bishops may in fact act as organizers of Christian life and action; indeed this may often be demanded by historical circumstances. However, this does not seem to be as essential to their function in the Church as is their guidance of such life and action through their witness to faith.

It seems, then, that the very nature of the Church as a community of faith and sacramental worship requires the ministry exercised by the episcopacy. If this be true, the episcopal college — with the responsibility, authority, and function we have described — is an indispensable element of continuity in the Church's social structure.

This does not mean that the particular ecclesiastical structures with which we are familiar, and through which the episcopacy guides the Church at present, are essential to the Church. Parishes, dioceses as large organizational units, the Roman curia: all of these are the result of practical judgments made earlier in history. They were established as means through which the ministry of the bishops could effectively form Christians into a community. As such they are necessarily subject to judgment; they must be appraised, modified, or abandoned, insofar as they effectively achieve (or do not achieve) their purpose. Each historical and cultural situation must establish those structures of community life which make it possible for Christians to become increasingly a community of faith and worship and apostolic endeavor through the sacramental influence of the episcopal college.

Ours is apparently one of those historical situations in which a large-scale revamping of ecclesiastical structures is demanded. Unprecedented mobility marks our contemporary life. Men and women find themselves involved in many human communities other than the neighborhood relationship that formerly constituted their entire context of relationships. Modern communications media and computers have changed the pattern of gathering and imparting knowledge. The Church is faced with the need to find those patterns of Christian life and activity which will express Christianity's deepest traditions in the midst of this explosively developing world. One of the most important aspects of the task facing the Church is the relationship between bishops and people. Structures must be found which enable the episcopacy to exert its true leadership in faith and worship, so that bishops and people together can form a Christian community capable of bringing Christ's redeeming influence to the lives of men.

Whether it be in the credal formulations of her faith, or in the liturgical forms of her sacramental worship, or in the organized structures of her community life, the contemporary Church is faced with the inescapable need to confront the question of continuity and discontinuity. Both history and the New Testament writings indicate the peril and the promise of this enterprise. Both also indicate that such an undertaking is intrinsic to the nature of the Church, which is a living reality, an eschatological community still growing into the full maturity destined for it, a pilgrim people on the way to the true promised land.

CHAPTER FOUR

Word of God
or Words of Men

HISTORY MAY well record the 1960s as one of the most productive ten years of mankind's religious thought. Vatican II and the two meetings of the World Council of Churches, at New Delhi and Uppsala, were the occasion for a vast number of books and articles, as well as innumerable conferences and lectures. Not all the theological effort of these years was important, but a considerable amount was; genuine theological advance occurred in almost every branch of Christian thought. And somewhat the same was happening outside Christianity.

Strangely enough, one of the most-discussed groups of thinkers during this period apparently challenged the very possibility of any genuine religious thought. The so-called "death of God" theologians contested not only the relative adequacy of theological reflection but the reality of any object (i.e. God) towards which theology could direct itself. The position espoused by these men was not entirely new, for it grew out of the questions raised by modern agnosticism. Like the earlier agnostic thinkers — Feuerbach, Marx, Nietzsche, Freud — the "death of God" theologians are suggesting the demise, not of God, but of religion. Their criticisms are directed at the manner in which men have thought about the divine and fashioned their lives and religious practices accordingly.

The Limitations of Language

It is both interesting and significant that much of the discussion raised by the "death of God" theologians deals with the question of religious language. They are not alone in this interest in the words that men use to explain their faith and their understanding of the God they worship. In one way or another, every theologian today must deal with the question of interpreting the language used in Scripture, in worship, in theological reflection, and in people's everyday expression of their religious understandings. Nor is this entirely new. For many centuries theologians have examined the validity and appropriateness of the words used in speaking about the divine.

Today, however, the discussion of religious language is more intense, and is part of the contemporary preoccupation with the problem of personal communication. At the very time when men have developed unprecedented media of human communications — radio, TV, and others — we have become more acutely aware of the grave obstacles that bar true communication in many areas of life. This is not just a question of the increasing complexity of information, or of the fact that specialized knowledges have grown so technical and sophisticated that the ordinary person is incapable of understanding the words (or other symbols) employed by the experts.

What is more disconcerting is our discovery of the extent to which all language is inadequate. Particularly when there is question of conveying understanding from one person to another, language is very limited. Even when people live in the same culture, speak the same language, have basically the same experiences, it is difficult for them to find words that express accurately their deepest human feelings and attitudes. The problem becomes more acute when people from different cultures deal with one another, as is increasingly the case in our world.

Like men of previous generations, we strive to overcome part of this defect of ordinary language by using special media:

poetry, movies, art, dance. Unlike earlier generations, we do
all this much more self-consciously; and we become ever
more aware of how alienated we are from one another, from
the physical universe we attempt to understand and master,
and from the transcendent reality we call "God." The general
problem of the inadequacy of language finds a more intense
application in religious language. What human words could
possibly be the means for describing the reality of God, who
by definition is beyond human comprehension? On the other
hand, what human words could be the medium through
which the divinity manifested himself to men? Both revelation
(God's word to men) and worship (man's word to God)
seem to be impossible, or at least so lacking in accuracy as to
be seriously misleading.

Yet the use of language is unavoidable; we humans are
language-using beings. Granting all the difficulties of finding
relatively adequate words for many occasions, language is essential to all human communication and therefore to all
human community. Without words to share our human feelings and ideas, we would find it impossible to form friend-
ships. Without the use of words for such things as laws, it
would be impossible for nations and other organized human
societies to exist.

Human life, because it is personal, it necessarily "dialogic."
We must converse with one another, or we could not become
aware of each other or even of ourselves. Such converse is the
very basis of our presence to one another. Thus, with all the
difficulties involved, we necessarily search for meaningful
ways of responding to one another. We search for a better
understanding of the language that we use, and we search for
less inadequate language.

All of this highlights the problem of religion. If religion
means anything, it means some relationship between men and
the divinity. If this relationship is to be in any sense personal,
there must be some possibility of "dialogue" between men
and God. In some fashion, God must be able to speak to
men, men must be able to speak to one another about God,

and they must be able to express in words their attitude towards God.

If such communication between men and God is utterly impossible, religion can be nothing other than a projection of men's need to find some ultimate frame of reference, some horizon for their experience, which can provide integration for human experience. Such subjective "creation" of a divinity to fit men's psychological needs might conceivably remove some fears from life, it might inject some ultimate meaning into the enigmatic happenings of man's existence, it might give men the strength "to carry on"; but in reality it would be illusion, and the discovery of its unreality would be shattering to men individually and socially. Should religion prove to be nothing more than this, it should be attacked as ultimately harmful to man and should be banished from human life. This, of course, has been the suggestion of certain prominent modern thinkers.

Those who profess religion as a genuine reality, who believe that it is grounded in reality both on the divine and on the human side of the relationship between men and God, must take seriously the function of religious language. And if careful analysis must be made of the ordinary words that religious men use to describe their relation to God, special attention must be paid to the Bible, because those religious groups that ground their faith and worship in the Bible believe that it is in unique fashion the "word of God." Human language records the religious experience of the Old Testament people and of the early Christians, but Christian faith sees the language as more than that; it considers the text of the Bible as "inspired," as a true medium through which God speaks to men.

But how can the human language used in the Scriptures be truthfully called "word of God"? In attempting to answer this question, it would be good to determine, if possible, the process by which God communicated with men during the period when the texts of the Bible were produced. Whatever this process was (and obviously it was not one of God using human words to speak, since he is not human), if it did result in an understanding by men of God, we can call it "word."

The people of Israel, and Christians who identify with Israel's faith, believe that God spoke to men in the actions that he performed on Israel's behalf. Both Israel and Christianity look upon the happenings of Israel's life as "salvation history," and Christians see this historical process as finding its culmination in the life, death, and resurrection of Jesus of Nazareth. This is another way of saying that God revealed himself, i.e. "spoke," to men through the deeds he performed on the behalf of men.

This is a way of speaking that is familiar to us. We often look upon it, in fact, as the most authentic way of giving expression to our ideas and attitudes. We are very conscious that a spoken word can be easily uttered, but that our actions often give a more solid indication of what we really think — actions speak louder than words. We recognize that the actions performed by a person are a translation of his intentions and attitudes. The Old Testament people and the primitive Christian community justifiably interpreted the events of their experience as an indication of God's attitude towards them. They saw those events as "words" which revealed God himself — as Yahweh in the Old Testament, as the Father of Jesus Christ for the early Christians.

The Word of Yahweh

Leaving aside for the moment the precise manner in which God guided the historical happenings of Israel's history, if he did so guide it (and this is the belief of both Israel and Christianity), the course of that history would indicate for us the attitude of God toward men. It would speak the divine intent toward men.

In this perspective, it seems highly significant that the general movement of Israel's history is one of progressive liberation, a movement from servitude to freedom. This movement is found in the first formative event of Old Testament history: the liberation of the people from Egyptian servitude. But it also finds expression in the slow but unmistakable evolution of religious responsibility among the people of Israel; in the gradually emerging consciousness that they must accept responsibility for their decisions; in their recognition of the burden as well as the dignity of freedom. In this movement of history the "word" of Yahweh seems to be his desire that men be free, that they determine their own history and destiny, that they increasingly accept with maturity their personhood. This desire also speaks the divine intent to deal with men on a personal basis. Men are not "things" he has made, they are persons to whom he wishes to relate in friendship.

Again, the whole thrust of Old Testament history seems to be one in which the people are led from childhood to maturity. If this is a God-guided and purposeful history, then the "word" of Old Testament revelation is that Yahweh desires his people to make their own decisions, to come to grips with the circumstances of life, and not to await some miraculous intervention on his part to solve their problems.

The reality of God and of his dynamic presence to his people is itself a "message" to Israel. It says that they are his "chosen people"; that his watchful providence cares for them and protects them from their enemies; that he is an "interested" God and not some capricious and domineering force. Moreover, the kind of divinity he is and the relationship he has established with Israel demands a certain kind of response from the people, both in their social life and in their worship.

Because the Israelites were human beings, with human ways of understanding, this basic reality of a God who acts had to be expressed in ideas and words. Only through such words and the ideas they express are men able to make intelligible the events of life that they experience. The experience that the Old Testament people had in faith needed to be formulated in ideas and words. The precise forms of thought and language into which the experience of the revealing God were cast were those proper to ancient Israel's cultural and historical situation.

We do not know the exact process by which Old Testament Israel came into being as the people of Yahweh. We do know that an essential role in this process was played by the ancient traditions that described the exodus, the role of Moses, the desert wanderings, the Sinai covenant, the entry into the promised land. Among these traditions the beginnings of the law played a key role. The law spelled out for the people the will of their God, guided the formation of the people as a social and religious entity, gave expression to faith's insight into the meaning and purpose of Israel.

Over the decades and centuries, these words of tradition were safeguarded and transmitted from one generation to another. They were considered as more than just human words of recollection; They were "word of God," communicated to the people through charismatic figures like Moses, a guide to Israel's self-understanding and a norm for Israel's actions. Whether or not one accepts Israel's belief that this guidance actually came from God (to assent to that belief is a judgment of faith), the historical fact is clear: These sacred traditions of the Old Testament people actually did function in a most important way in shaping the mentality and behavior of Israel. The Israelites thought of themselves as the people chosen by Yahweh; they felt themselves bound by his laws; they lived with a sense of his guiding and protecting presence.

For the people of ancient Israel, the word of Yahweh was much more than a word of explanation, much more than a detailed code of moral behavior. The word of Yahweh was a word of power; it was able to effect that which it said; it transmitted life and power to Israel. It was a word of promise: It brought blessing to those who accepted and followed it, it brought punishment to those who neglected or rejected it. It existed in the midst of the people as a constant witness to Israel's election by Yahweh, as a witness to the covenant that linked Yahweh and the people, as a witness to the saving will of Yahweh. It was the sign, the "sacrament," just as were shrine and Temple, of Yahweh's powerful and demanding presence.

Actually, shrine and word of tradition functioned closely together in making Yahweh present to the faith of the people. There are many indications that the ancient shrines — and eventually the Temple in Jerusalem — played a key role in developing and preserving Israel's sacred traditions. The word of liturgical celebration embraced the words of law and religious recollection. The liturgy itself was a word, a communication to the participants about their identity and responsibility as Yahweh's elect. And it was in conjunction with liturgy that much of the verbal formulation of Israel's traditions must have taken place.

When we reflect on the process of Israel's emergence as a people, we can see the power exerted by this "word of Yahweh" that was proposed to the people for their faith-acceptance. Even in the primitive stages of the traditions, this word began to mold the thinking of the loosely-federated tribes, slowly forming a common heritage and consciousness, gradually bringing into existence a community of faith. Israel was a people formed by the word of God.

In speaking this way, however, one must be careful not to overlook the full scope of "Yahweh's word" according to the Old Testament understanding of it. Though verbal formulations became more ample, more complex, and more canonized by official usage, the basic "word" that still spoke to the conscience of Israel was Yahweh's saving action, that reality to which the words of tradition tried to give expression. Even when the various traditions were finally gathered together into the Old Testament Scriptures, Israel never became a "people of the book." The word of God remained always a continuing and dynamic process. God continued in each generation to speak through the events of Israel's historical experience.

One can see this process sharply exemplified in the case of Israel's great charismatic prophets. They were keenly aware of the traditions of Israel's faith, and much of their endeavor was directed to recalling the people to observance of these traditions. At the same time, they were dominated by aware-

ness of the power of Yahweh's word as it spoke through them
to the people. The classic form of prophetic oracle is always
in the present tense: "Thus says the Lord God. . . ."

It is in the prophetic tradition that we see most clearly Israel's belief that the word of Yahweh is a word of power. The
word of God is inescapable; once expressed through the
mouth of the prophet it goes forth to accomplish the will of
Yahweh. One of the clearest expressions of this power attached to the prophetic word — which is really Yahweh's
word — is found in the opening chapter of the book of Jeremiah, which describes the vocation of the prophet. In his call
to the prophetic function, a call that Jeremiah is reluctant to
accept, the prophet is told that the word placed on his lips will
be effective of either blessing or curse; this word will bring both
life and death.

The prophetic word has such power precisely because it is
directed to the present moment. Situated at a given moment in
the historical experience of his people, the prophet addresses
himself to his fellow-Israelites so they may understand the
true dimensions of the life which they have at that moment.
His word is a word of explanation, an explanation that is
rooted not in human insight and shrewdness, but in Yahweh's
own communication to his people. It is the reality and saving
activity of Yahweh that alone explains the life situation of Israel at any point in its history. This is the explanation that
comes through the prophetic oracle. It is much more than a
literary form, then, when the prophet begins his exhortation
with the words: "Thus says the Lord God . . . ."

In assessing the implications of their own historical circumstances, the prophets drew from the deepest currents of Israel's traditions. Because Yahweh's past deeds indicated his
lasting love for his people, they constituted a promise that
Yahweh in his fidelity to Israel would certainly fulfill. But the
word of God that was on the lips of the prophets was a word
that was meant to direct the consciousness of Israel toward
the future; it was a word that called them to action — more

precisely to conversion. What the prophetic oracle demanded of Old Testament Israel was a decision, a decision for Yahweh.

The power of God's word, then, was a power that acted in conjunction with human freedom. If received in faith and openness, this word could vivify and strengthen Israel. Refusal of this word would lead to destruction and death, as it did for the northern kingdom in 722, and for Jerusalem in 586.

Our tendency in reflecting upon the mystery of Yahweh's word and its impact on Israel's history is to consider its influence in psychological terms: It shaped and stimulated the consciousness of the Old Testament people, guiding them to that course of action which would realize Israel's historical destiny. While Israel's prophets were certainly aware of this psychological aspect of Yahweh's word — after all, they lived and preached under the "possession" of this word — they looked upon this word as something almost physical. It was a cosmic power that directed the happenings of nature and history.

Yahweh's word, as the prophets thought about it, was an irresistible force unleashed in the world, and the prophet was the agency through which the word entered into the life of men. While the word was not identical with Yahweh himself, it bore the power of his own person and it effected his will. The word was what made Yahweh present to the people he had chosen, and the prophet was the tangible sign of this presence. Though he might be an irritant in the midst of men who disliked being shaken from their complacency and self-centeredness, though he might be resented by those of the "establishment" whom he challenged and attacked, the prophet was still a sign of Yahweh's fidelity to his people.

One could really speak of the prophetic word as "sacramental"; it truly made Yahweh present in the midst of his people. It was not a word about God; it was God's own word, it was true personal communication from him to his beloved people, it was his means of giving himself to this people.

Small wonder, then, that the faith-community of Israel cherished and preserved the words of the prophets as a part of its sacred traditions. Yet, in a way, this preservation was a wonder, for the prophets generally received less than enthusiastic acceptance from their contemporaries. The message they spoke was often not what men wished to hear, and most of the prophets received only from later generations the acceptance and veneration that had been denied to them in their own lifetimes.

More important than this posthumous vindication of the prophet was the fact that his prophetic oracles were preserved, so that they might guide later generations as they tried to puzzle out the word that God was speaking to them through their own historical circumstances. While the prophet addressed himself to his own contemporaries and his words dealt with the concrete realities of a given historical moment, these words also contained something of the eternal because they spoke for the eternal God and about his unchanging love for men.

While we generally associate Israel's theological reflection about the word of Yahweh with the prophetic movement, it was not just the prophets who possessed a developed "theology of the word." Both in the priestly tradition and in the Deuteronomic elements of the Old Testament we find a sophisticated theological treatment of the word, of the power it exercises in the cosmos and in human history, of its role as bearer of life and mediator of Yahweh's will.

In the first part of Genesis, which derives from the priestly tradition, the word of Yahweh is the medium of creation. The Lord God spoke, and there was light. He spoke again and there was the structured world, and life — and finally man. In ancient literature it is difficult to find an equally spiritual and exalted description of the origin of the universe. It is the intrinsic power of the divine command that, in the view of Israel's theologians, brought created reality into existence and sustains it.

We can recapture some of ancient Israel's understanding of

the law when we recall that it, too, is part of the mystery of Yahweh's powerful word. The giving of the law was basic to the formation of Israel as a people, and the progress or decline of the people's fortunes is directly dependent upon their observance or neglect of this law. When they describe the career of Israel as it stretches from the entry into the promised land to the Babylonian exile, a career that began with such promise and ends (at least temporarily) amid the tragedy of Jerusalem's destruction, the Deuteronomic historians explain the rise and fall of Israel in terms of Yahweh's word. When the people, and particularly the kings, observe the laws of Yahweh, there is peace and prosperity. When they refuse to listen to Yahweh, they are powerless and fall before their enemies.

All ancient peoples were intrigued by the phenomena of order and power (particularly, the power of life) that they observed on all sides. They attempted to give some explanation of these phenomena through their myths. Israel's theologians, though they were aware of these myths of surrounding cultures, found their own explanation in terms of Yahweh's word. This word was the source of both life and order in the world of nature and in human society.

Like other ancient peoples, Israel, too, saw that both life and order were constantly threatened by the mysterious negative force of evil and chaos. Here, also, Israel's thinkers introduce the idea of the word. Yahweh's word is in conflict with the power of chaos at the creation of the world, at the occurrence of disasters like the great flood, when Israel's life as a people is threatened by the disruptions of war, or when Israel's own internal existence in peace and justice is threatened by the people's sinfulness.

Life and death applied to Israel as a people; they also applied to each man and woman in Israel. The word of Yahweh which came through law and prophet had to be received in faith by the people as a whole and by each individual within the people. The truly wise man was the one who listened to the guidance that was provided by Yahweh's word. He had learned the secret to life, for the word to which he was attentive was the source of both life and wisdom. How much wiser could a man be than to be wise with God's own wisdom? Certainly, there was no surer path to life.

With such an appreciation of the importance of Yahweh's word, it was logical for Israel to cherish the traditions of what God had spoken to her through the events of her history, through the law, and through the prophets. This the Israelites did over many centuries, gradually giving expression to the traditions in written form, and slowly gathering them into the collection we know as the Bible.

Long before the full form of the Old Testament Scriptures came into existence, the various elements of the Bible were already having a major impact on the faith and life of the people. Generation after generation of the Israelites drew from these sacred writings to interpret the happenings of their own day, to understand better their own identity as a chosen people, and to gain courage in the face of the adversities they faced. It was these sacred writings that played a large role in transmitting the faith of Israel from father to son, and in safeguarding the integrity of Yahweh's word in the course of that transmission.

Just as the shrine-situations had contributed so much to the early preservation and development of Israel's traditions, and thereby led to the production of the Bible, so in the later period of Old Testament history it is chiefly in such worship-contexts that people came into contact with the Scriptures. In the centuries that followed the Babylonian exile, the synagogue service probably consisted in readings from the law and the prophets. In this way, the word of God that had come to the people of Israel throughout the centuries continued to mold the faith of the people, and to give them direction in their lives.

To the very end of the historical period we refer to as Old Testament times, the word of God had a wider extension than the written Scriptures. In each generation, the Israelites believed, Yahweh continued to work with his people and the events of their experience were still a medium in which they ascertained his will. The Bible served as a privileged guide to understanding the significance and practical imperatives of life, but the understanding of the Bible itself was affected by the historical circumstances in which later generations of Jews found themselves. Scripture and life interacted to communicate God's will to his people.

What the religious experience of the Old Testament people seems to show is that the basic revelation, the basic word, the basic event, is Israel herself. This people, whose life of faith stretches over more than a millenium, is itself the manifestation of Yahweh's saving activity and therefore of his loving intent towards men. For each generation of Israelites, their religious traditions spoke to them about this event-word as it had found expression in the lives of their ancestors. But for each generation, their own experience of what it meant to be Israel played a central role in their faith.

So, too, for those faith-communities — Christian or Jewish — which today accept the Old Testament Scriptures as "word of God," the word that speaks to them in faith is not primarily the text of the Bible. It is the faith-experience of Old Testament Israel, as expressed in the biblical text, which helps present-day believers to understand more deeply their own encounter with this God who acts in human history to save men. It would be naive fundamentalism to look in the experience of Israel for exact parallels to our own life-situation. But there are two elements of sameness that link us with the Old Testament people: our common humanity, and our common faith in this God who acts with unchanging and redeeming love.

The Word of Jesus

For Christians, there is another word they can use to interpret both their understanding of Old Testament Israel and their own experience of life in a community of faith. This word is Jesus of Nazareth, whom Christian faith accepts as the incarnation of God the Father's own Word, his own Son.

Since its earliest days, Christianity has seen Jesus as the final and fulfilling word of Old Testament revelation. All the writings of the New Testament are dominated by this view. In Jesus, who is the Christ (the Messiah of Old Testament expectation), there is realized all that God had been doing for his people during the preceding centuries. His teaching is the fulfillment of Old Testament prophecy and the highest expression of Israel's wisdom movement. As law-giver he is superior even to Moses himself.

All that went into the saving history of Israel was preparation for and promise of this definitive saving event, the life and death and resurrection of the Christ. All the great figures of Old Testament times — Moses, David, Solomon, the prophets — prefigured this man Jesus, and by their lives and activities prepared for the understanding of the word God spoke in Jesus. All the institutions of Old Testament life and religion — law, temple, kingship, priesthood — find their true meaning when they are seen as preparations for him who will institute the new people of God through his death and resurrection.

While there is a pattern and progression in the historical evolution of Israel, the true direction of that evolution is seen only when the goal of Old Testament history, Jesus of Nazareth, is revealed to men as Messiah and Lord. Elements of Old Testament life that had never found an adequate reconciliation with one another, like kingship and prophecy, find an unexpected synthesis by being fulfilled simultaneously in Jesus, the Christ. Without distorting or depreciating the intrinsic word of Old Testament revelation, Christian faith believes that there is a level of meaning in this word spoken to Israel that becomes known only with Christ.

In Jesus of Nazareth, God speaks all that he has to say to men, for Jesus is his own infinite Word; that word having been spoken, there is really nothing more to say. However, it might be good to note quickly something we will examine later in more detail. It is really not accurate to say "that word having been spoken," because from the moment of Jesus' human conception the Father continues to speak his Word to men unendingly. The Incarnation is not a past mystery, it is a constantly present event.

What the incarnating of the Son in Jesus means is that God is speaking himself humanly. A medium of communication is established in which men can truly come into personal contact with divinity. This does not mean simply that Jesus, as the Father's Word, can talk with privileged insight about the reality of God. Rather, all that he is and does as man gives utterance to the reality of God and of God's love for men. Jesus is what it means for God to exist humanly and in familiar identification with men. Jesus is what it means for a man to live as son in relation to the heavenly Father.

Jesus' life, and particularly his death and resurrection, is the unique event of salvation history that constitutes the underlying "word" from God to men which human words then strive, always inadequately, to express. What God does in Jesus of Nazareth reveals what kind of God he is: He is the Father of our Lord, Jesus Christ. This is the identity of the Father as person, and this means that in Jesus we can truly know *who* God is.

If Christian faith in Jesus as the incarnated Word of the Father is true, the notion of "revelation" takes on a new and added level of significance. Jesus himself is the supreme revelation, and because he relates as a "self" to his fellow-men, bringing us into conscious contact with his Father as a "self," revelation is clearly a divine action of self-giving. No level of God's dealings with men is more mysterious. God is not only the creator who puts all reality in existence and preserves it, not only the loving creator who guides men's lives and fortunes. Inexplicably, he chooses to be Father to men, linking them in the bond of a common humanity with his own Son. Thereby, without threat to his transcendence, he is personally involved in the experience and destiny of all mankind.

Such a conclusion might seem utterly presumptuous, even preposterous. Yet, one need only read the Gospel parable which describes God as the father of the prodigal son, in order to see that this is the ancient faith of the Church, rooted in the teaching of Jesus himself (Lk. 15:11-32). No one can read in that parable how the father of the errant prodigal went out to watch for the return of his son, and then think of God as an infinite and transcendent divinity incapable of deep personal involvement in the lives of his children.

Revelation and divine presence become clearly and totally identified in Christ. Jesus is the manifestation of the Word; he is also the sacrament of the Father's presence (Jn. 1:14; 14:9). Persons become fully present to one another when each in his consciousness is open to the words spoken by the other: each becomes present in the other's awareness, and it is here that he reveals himself. As no other human possibly could, Jesus was open to this kind of self-giving on the part of his Father. Jesus' human consciousness was the human expression of the Father's very self-utterance, his Word. We are incapable of fathoming the reality of this mystery, but we can grasp enough to see how it constituted a situation of unparalleled personal intimacy and presence.

But the mystery of God's self-revealing presence does not stop with Jesus of Nazareth. Through him it is meant to reach out to all men and women, for Jesus is the Word expressed humanly. The very finality of Christ's human existing is communication; the very being and purpose of words is to be a medium of communication. The intrinsic purpose of Jesus being man is to be his Father's word of revelation. Everything he is and does as man is directed to the goal of bringing men and his Father into deepened personal relationship. He speaks for his Father to men, and he speaks for men to his Father.

Being man, however, Jesus had to utilize human words in order to realize his purpose. Without words, he could not have shared with his contemporaries the vision of reality, human and divine, that was his. Without words, he could not even have had truly human consciousness of himself in the midst of human experience, for language is indispensable for human thinking. But words were ultimately incapable of speaking the revelation that he was. He could reveal himself and his Father only by the supreme self-giving of his death and resurrection.

Jesus' death and resurrection is, then, the supreme word spoken by a man to his fellow-men. So rich in significance is it, that all else in human existence is interpreted by it. The entire course of human history will be needed to spell out its implications. All else that Jesus said and did was preparation for understanding this, his ultimate human self-expression, his ultimate personal self-giving to his brethren.

However, it would be a mistake to see the earlier words of Jesus as nothing more than anticipation. They formed part of the action of redeeming revelation which came to full statement in his passage through death into new life. Jesus did not wait until the Last Supper to begin his saving work. This work began with his entry into humanity, with his becoming man. It took on a fuller expression with his public ministry, which itself led directly into the events of Holy Week.

As the Gospels describe it, the public ministry of Jesus already manifested the power of his words, the power that derived from his identity as the Word. Most of Jesus' activity consisted in teaching, and apparently his hearers recognized the special authority possessed by his words, though they did not grasp the full scope of this authority (Mt. 7:28-29). On the most obvious level, his words had the power of communicating to men a new vision of life, a vision dominated by the reality of his Father's concern for men.

While we have few, if any, direct citations from Jesus' own public teaching, there is no reason for denying that the New Testament writings put us in essential contact with the message that Jesus conveyed to his hearers. Reading the Gospels in this light, we are unable to miss the constant insistence on the reality of his Father's loving concern for men. The Sermon on the Mount is but one, though perhaps the most striking, example in this regard. Practically all the parables have as their purpose to describe the true nature and activity of his heavenly Father.

Directly, such teaching is intended to convey an understanding of the Father. Indirectly, it points out the true nature of human life and destiny. Man as the beloved of God is meant to pass from this present life into unending possession of joy and peace, into eternal life with God. Many of the images used in the parables describe God as gathering men to himself: the shepherd with his sheep, the farmer gathering the harvest into his barns, the king inviting guests into his banquet, the net cast into the sea. In some passages this action is stated in more direct fashion: "No one can come to me unless the Father who sent me draws him" (Jn. 6:44). Jesus is depicted as describing his own role in these same terms: "I, when I am lifted up from the earth, will draw all men to myself" (Jn. 12:32).

There seems to be little doubt that Jesus' words had great effect on people. True, the bulk of the people gradually drifted away from him as the import of his teaching began to be realized. But his following was important enough to win the enmity of the leaders of the Jews and to lead to his death. Moreover, in the centuries since his death, the teaching of Jesus has provided insight and inspiration for countless millions of men and women, even for many who could not accept the full mystery of his divine identity, and who for this reason never embraced the Christian faith.

The pages of the New Testament books indicate, however, that the early Christians believed in the power of Christ's words beyond their ability to influence men's minds. Like the prophetic word of old, though more so, the words of Jesus had power over the very forces of the physical universe (Mt. 8:26). His wondrous deeds of healing and giving life are almost always described in terms of his verbal command: "Young man, I say to you, arise" (Lk. 7:14). His words call the dead to life, they cure paralytics, they give sight to the blind. At the same time, it should be noted, these words arouse faith, and if there is no faith to receive his word, there is no healing.

Like the word of Yahweh as it is described in the first

chapter of Genesis, the word of Jesus is directed against the power of chaos. In the world of his day, as in our own, the enigmatic force of evil and chaos was felt in many areas of human life. Ignorance, error, and prejudice darkened the minds of men, touching even their religious faith. Physical disabilities of all kinds made the lives of many a constant experience of suffering and discouragement. In the social sphere, injustice and exploitation deprived large segments of the populace of the dignity and freedom that was their birthright as humans and as members of a covenant people. Most deeply, men and women were touched by the evil of their own sinfulness.

Jesus' words, as the Gospels indicate, were directed against evil in all its diverse forms. His teaching was aimed at overcoming the false understandings his hearers had, above all the falsification that had crept into their self-understanding as the chosen people. Gentle toward the common people who unquestioningly went along with the religious instruction that had been given them, Jesus harshly denounced the religious leaders who were misrepresenting the Old Testament word of God and imposing heavy burdens on the consciences of people (Mt. 23).

In much the same vein, he attacked the social exploitation of the poor and uninstructed. Nor was this only an attack on the economic injustices under which many suffered. Jesus' teaching was directed at that subtle type of psychic destruction which takes place among deprived people when they accept the snobbish judgment of a society that evaluates them as less important persons than the rich and the powerful. The public teaching of Jesus catches up one of the most prominent themes of later Old Testament thought, the praise of the "little ones of Yahweh" (Mt. 11:25). It is the "poor in spirit," not the rich and influential, who are blessed (Mt. 5:3).

To digress for a moment, it is remarkable how this approach of Jesus anticipates some of our most recent insights into the needs of deprived minorities. Only in the past few

years have we realized how critical to the self-betterment of
deprived groups is the discovery of their own human dignity.
Without this attitude economic subsidies and employment op-
portunities are unable to guide these people to genuine social
equality. Men and women must appreciate their own personal
worth before they trust themselves enough to become decisive
masters of their own life-patterns and destinies.

Numerous passages in the Gospels describe the healing
power of Jesus' words. They touched the sensible ailments of
the body, but they reached more profoundly to heal the sin
that afflicts man's spirit. One could, of course, read such passages and understand Jesus' activity as almost magical. This
would be a serious misreading of his activity as the Father's
incarnated Word. What he speaks is his Father's saving love;
it is this love that directly opposes the evil of sin. Love is the
contradiction of sin and is the only force able to overcome
sin. Jesus' words transmit this love — his Father's and his
own — to the consciousness and affectivity of his hearers. In
men's free response to this word their adherence to sin is bro-
ken.

There is one more aspect of Jesus' words that we might examine briefly, before we go on to study the mystery of God's
word in our present world. This is the power of his word to
form community. Here, too, his activity stands in continuity
with the functioning of Yahweh's word in Old Testament history. Whether it was the word of the law, or the word of liturgy, the word of the wise man, or the word of prophet, Israel's acceptance of this word as ultimately coming from
Yahweh united the people into a community of faith. Without
the communication of Yahweh's word as Israel believed in it,
there would have been no people of Israel. Whether one
judges them wise or deluded in their belief that God spoke to
them in the events of their life and through the charismatic
mediators he sent to them, the fact remains that this faith was
the basis for Israel's existence as a distinctive historical entity.

Jesus comes as the Word incarnated, so that he can bring
to fulfillment this work of establishing human community. In

its scope his work extends far beyond the horizons of Israel, for the community to be formed by the incarnate Word is the entire family of mankind: "Go therefore and make disciples of all nations . . ." (Mt. 28:19). Human community in the true sense, men genuinely sharing life in common, is necessarily grounded in a shared vision of what life is. Such a vision was communicated by Jesus in his public teaching, confirmed in his death and resurrection, and cherished by his disciples as the bond of their unity.

True human community is also dependent upon love and concern for one another among those in the community. Without this, there can be no personal dimension to the societies that men form; they can organize together for economic or military advantage, they can cooperate in scientific research for purely selfish aims, but they cannot constitute authentic human community. Here we can see the power of Jesus' words, for the message he bears is that of love for men, his own love and his Father's love, to which men must respond by their love for one another (Jn. 13:34).

Exalted as the goal of universal human community is, the power of Christ's word reaches out beyond this. As the Father's own Word, as the medium of communication between God and men, the intrinsic role of Jesus is that of forming a community which embraces both God and men. The mystery of personal community revealed to us in the incarnation of the Word is the extension of that community in life which is the unity of God. By his word, the Father reaches out to share himself with men and unite them to himself.

The Word of God Today

Jesus' words, then, were words of power, a power grounded in his own identity as the Father's Word. But the believer today can justifiably ask the question: How does this presence of God's word in Jesus of Nazareth touch me? Is there anything more than the cherished memory of the teaching of Jesus which can serve as some guide for life today?

Does God still speak in our own day and, if so, does he still speak in Jesus of Nazareth?

To these questions Christian faith responds with a clear answer: The word of God is a continuing reality in our present world. God still speaks to men. Revelation is not just a past happening, of which we have a record in the pages of Scripture; it is an event that still takes place in and through the lives and faith of men today. Recent theological thought, both Catholic and Protestant, has increasingly drawn attention to this contemporary aspect of the word of God, and Vatican II stressed it in its decree on divine revelation.

To give some meaning to this contention that God still speaks to us today, we must examine several aspects of this continuing divine revelation. There is the question of the manner in which the Bible still functions as word of God. Closely allied with this question is the role of Christian sacraments as media of revelation. There is also the function of the Christian community, in the totality of its life and faith, as a manifestation of God's self-giving to mankind. And beyond this, the whole life-experience of men is a "word" from God.

In many ways, this last form of "the word of God" is the most basic and inclusive communication from God to men. If one accepts the faith of Christianity and Judaism (as well as of other religions, like Islam) in the providential influence of God in human life, it follows that the realities of each man's life are somehow meant to speak to him. Each man or woman is faced with a distinctive life-situation that is unrepeatable. Each of us has his own personality and capabilities; each of us bears a certain heritage of family and culture and education; each of us lives in the midst of a given group of people. All of this speaks to us the possibilities of achievement, the possibilities of our growth as persons, the possibilities of making the world a better situation for ourself and others. All of this lays on us certain responsibilities, to ourselves and to others.

Nor does the life-situation of each of us remain a static

word. It is constantly being modified by the various events that make up our human life-experience. In our own lifetime, the rapid advance of scientific discovery and of technology, the almost unbelievable breakthroughs in communications media, the disaster of global war, have both increased and limited the potential for human development which is ours. How much greater, for example, would be the possibility of bringing true promise of human development to those now oppressed by utter poverty, if the staggering amounts of money spent on war and armaments could somehow be devoted to overcoming poverty. Were that done, life would have a quite different meaning for these impoverished human beings; life would speak a different word than it now does.

If one believes in the creative and providential influence of God in his life, it means that one is not accidentally in the situation that is his. True, this situation evolved out of myriad influences, many of them decisions made by himself or by other human beings; God has not acted by miraculous intervention to place us where we are. At the same time, Christian faith — as we find it expressed, for example, in the Sermon on the Mount — does see all this as somehow guided by the loving care of God. In this perspective, the actual life-context of each man is not only a given reality with which he must maturely deal, it is a gift to be accepted with gratitude.

Men have always puzzled, and still puzzle, over the word that life speaks to them. Many have seen life as expressing the will of God for them, but this can mean many things, dependent upon their understanding of God. If God is thought to be harshly oppressive, men can only view life with fear and resentment; if they think of God as mercifully watchful over mankind, they can live life with hope. Many men, of course, do not believe that human life derives any of its meaning from a relationship to God, for they either doubt or deny the reality of the divine. For such men, obviously, life can have no significance other than that which men themselves are able to give it, and not a few of these see man's existence as enigmatic and frustrating.

For Christians to claim that they see life as meaningful, with this meaning indicating the "will of God" for them, does not mean that they think the meaning of life is obvious. Even if one leaves aside for the moment the deeply enigmatic fact of evil, the complexities of our life, particularly in the modern world, are such that a man cannot decide easily what it is that he should do with his time and energies. Moreover, the various opinions regarding the meaning of life that are expressed in literature, philosophy, and popular communications media are so diverse that it can be hard to say what the "objective" meaning of life is.

And when one does take into account the evils that touch human existence today, it becomes almost impossible to give a satisfactory explanation for most men's lives. What purpose is served by the utter poverty of the bulk of mankind today; what good is accomplished by the fruitless attempt on the part of millions to eke out a miserable life? What possible meaning can one suggest for the suffering that comes to millions through disease, oppression, and war? When the greater proportion of men and women in the world have practically no hope of education or development of their human capabilities, what prospect of achievement can they have?

A Christian cannot, in the face of such realities, prate piously about God's providence. If he talks about providence, he must give this term a meaning that can at least suggest a true purpose for the human condition as it actually is. He can, of course, take refuge in the notion that God is acting in some totally mysterious way, and that despite what is happening in human history God will accomplish what he wishes. There may be some truth in the old adage that "God writes straight with crooked lines," but to see God's action as a bypassing of men's own activity is to make human life basically meaningless. As Christian faith understands divine providence, God's action does extend beyond what men can accomplish. Men need salvation, but God works with and through men. Men really do contribute effectively to the development of the human situation.

The Christian Conscience

If men are to work cooperatively with God for the genuine betterment of the world in which we live, it follows that they must somehow know what it is that God is striving to accomplish in the circumstances that make up their lives. This brings us back to our question: What is it that God is saying to us in and through the situation in which we find ourselves; what does this situation demand of us as a response? How is our contemporary world "word of God"?

One could ask another question: How does one form a genuine Christian conscience? At first sight, this seems to be a different query from the ones just asked; in actuality it is the same question. The word of God is addressed to men, who are not things but persons. As persons they are free, and this freedom interacts with whatever enters their conscious experience. Men hear what they wish to hear; their "discovery" of reality is strongly conditioned by their desires, by the decisions they have already made or are contemplating. Each of us, even when we strive to view life with open honesty and objectivity, must inevitably see reality from our own point of view.

Life speaks to us of the concrete demands and responsibilities laid upon us, but it can speak effectively only those demands we are willing to recognize. The demands of life are often general and undetermined; it is only through our choices that these demands become specific and determined. It is in these practical judgments, that is, in our conscience, that life as word of God speaks to us.

Conscience, then, is the ultimate medium through which reality speaks to men. By "conscience" we are, obviously, not referring to some mysterious "voice" that whispers to us a word of warning as we face decisions, or to a guilt feeling that follows upon some action. What we are describing is the judgment in which a course of action is determined as the appropriate one to follow. It is in such a judgment that the basic laws or dictates of human existence are applied to an individual and unique historical moment. This judgment constitutes for each man the ultimate law that he must follow. What each of us determines in a given set of circumstances to be the demands of life is at this point the effective demand laid upon us.

It is of critical importance that conscience be as correct as possible, that it reflect accurately the actualities of life. No more important task faces educators, particularly religious educators, than that of helping young people to develop a mature capacity for making honest and accurate judgments about their life-situations. Vatican II points to such careful formation of conscience as one of the most important responsibilities facing the Christian community at the present moment.

Such genuine formation of conscience is, of course, necessary to any authentic morality. But it is more than that; it is a necessary condition if men and women are to understand truthfully the meaning of themselves and of their world. A word conveys only that meaning which is admitted into the consciousness of the listener. The word that God speaks to men through the circumstances of their lives can only speak what they will allow it to speak. This is what the prophets of Israel realized when they castigated the men of their day for closing their ears to the word of Yahweh. This is what Jesus refers to when, in the Gospel account, he accuses the Jewish leadership of hypocritical blindness.

Honest willingness to face reality is fundamental to the process of conscience-judgment, but it does not suffice by itself. Correct understanding of life, of oneself, and of the world, is also necessary. Common sense, aided by the various disciplines of knowledge to which one is exposed in the course of his education, can provide much of this needed insight. But for the Christian there is an added need: How is he to discover that deeper dictate of life which flows from revelation; how is he to discover "the will of God"?

Scripture, Sacrament, Tradition

Christian faith sees three other elements interacting with life to form one mystery of "the word of God": the Old Testament and New Testament Scriptures, the actions of sacrament, the living tradition of the Christian community. Each of these says essentially the same thing, but each says it in its own way.

Most comprehensive and fundamental of these three complementary "words" is the Christian community in which the believer is situated and of which he himself is a member. Its living faith, to which the individual Christian is exposed in his family circle, in his reading and study, in his participation in liturgy, in his daily association with fellow Christians, is the primary criterion for his judgment about the reality of Christ, and his guide for understanding that reality.

Each Christian in his own lifetime contacts directly only a small portion of the worldwide community of faith. And, obviously, he contacts directly only this community as it exists today. Yet, the relatively small group each of us contacts immediately shares its faith and understanding with Christians throughout the world. And the Church of today shares the heritage of Christian faith with the Christians of previous centuries. Christians in all parts of the world and in all ages of history form one people of God, one believing community. They profess one common faith, though the precise manner of understanding and expressing that faith will vary in some respects from age to age and from one cultural situation to another.

It is this common faith of Christians, as we encounter it in its most recent formulation — the Church today — that speaks to each believer. It is truly a word that acts as a norm for the individual believer, clarifying for him, at the deeper level, the realities of life. This faith of the community reflects the action of the Holy Spirit, the action of Christ and his Father in our midst.

Within the Church, there is found a special norm for discerning the faith of the community. This is the episcopal college, the bishops of the world. Their unity in faith — with one another now, and with the bishops who have preceded them in the history of the Church — is a special sign, a sacrament in the full sense, of the Church's unity in faith. It is not as if the bishops can by themselves constitute a norm of faith, for their existence as a group can have meaning only in relation to the rest of the Christian community; but they are meant to serve within the entire Church as a visible guide for faith and therefore as a principle of Christian unity.

When we talk about "tradition" as a source and norm of faith, we sometimes tend to confine the meaning of the term to those official clarifications of faith, such as decrees of general councils, which come from the episcopacy. The term should have a wider meaning: It is the entire life of the Christian community — its formal teaching, its liturgical life, the daily experience of its members — as this develops organically over the centuries and transmits the mystery of Christ from one generation to another. It is this which speaks to the faith of each Christian the meaning of his life, of his world, and of the Church whose member he is.

While the faith of all preceding generations of Christians can and should act as a guide for our faith today, there is a special role that belongs to the very first generations of Christians, for they enjoyed a unique immediacy with the historical reality of Jesus. The close disciples of Jesus himself, as the witnesses of his public ministry and death and resurrection, obviously enjoyed an essential function in instructing the faith of the early Christians. On the foundation of their witness and teaching, and under the guidance of the Holy Spirit, the early Christian Church expressed her belief through the literature we call the New Testament. These writings, joined to the Old Testament Scriptures, have been accepted by the Christian community over the centuries as a privileged formulation of the revelation that takes place in Jesus of Nazareth. They are "word of God" in a manner unparalleled by any other religious literature.

By itself, however, the text of the Bible is not "word of God." The reality of the word of God, God communicating to men and revealing himself to them, takes place when in a living community of believers Scripture is proclaimed and heard, or read by a believer in the light of the faith he shares with the community. In this occurrence, the text, safeguarded and transmitted by the Church over the years, serves to formulate and unify the communication of God to men. By so doing, it gives shape to the faith and understanding of Christians and effects a basic congruence in the faith of believers over the centuries and throughout the world. It is an indispensable norm of authentic faith.

There are many elements in the Scriptures which are explicitly formulated precepts or value judgments or theological insights, and which, because they express some fundamental and universal truth, can serve directly as a criterion for Christians today as they evaluate their own life-situation. So rich is the Bible in such statements, that one can almost open the book at random and find a parable, or a psalm, or a proverb, or a prophetic oracle, that throws light on some aspect of life today. In this way, the Scriptures can act as a guide to men in understanding themselves and their world. As word of God the Bible helps indicate the deeper meaning of that word which God speaks to us through the circumstances of life.

Still, one must not view the Bible as just a collection of valuable sayings that can provide insights about God, man, and the world, or guidelines for conscience-judgments. There is a deeper level of insight and guidance that is meant to come through the Bible, precisely because it is the reflection of the religious experience of Old Testament Israel, of Jesus himself, and of early Christianity. It was in that experience, an experience of human life and consciousness touched by the revealing presence of God and transformed by faith, that God was revealed and the ultimate meaning of man's existence was explained.

While the actual historical circumstances of life were quite different for the people of Israel and for the early Christians than they are for us today, there is a basic course of human experience — birth, growth, joy and suffering, love, personal relationships in community, decision, sin and failure, death — which is common to men in all ages. In discovering how the mystery of God's revealing presence transformed the meaning of this basic experience in the lives of the people whose faith is expressed in the biblical writings, we today can gain invaluable insight into the manner in which our own experience is meant to be changed by faith in Christ. The experience of encounter with God in faith described in the pages of Scripture is meant to be word of God to men in all succeeding generations.

Most important is that transformation of human experience which occurred in the life, death, and resurrection of Jesus of Nazareth. In him is contained, in unique and unequalled fashion, that word about the meaning of human life which God revealed to men, for Jesus is the Father's own Word expressed humanly. In a manner we cannot understand, the human consciousness of Jesus was exposed to the reality of the divine, his Father. His human experience was truly human but transformed by the awareness of his Father. He is the exemplar for those who wish to live in the presence of God.

Jesus' human experience, as we find it reflected in the faith of the Christians who produced the New Testament literature, serves as an incomparable guide for Christians of all ages. Yet, the faith of the Church indicates that there is yet a deeper aspect to the mystery of Christ as word to men. As the risen Lord, Jesus remains present to men and especially to Christians; it is he himself, as the person he is, who challenges and changes men's understanding of life.

The analogue of human friendship is helpful here. If someone is a close friend of mine, we discuss many things together, and his insights and points of view exercise considerable influence on the way I think about myself and about life in general. He also "speaks" to me by being my friend. This tells me that I am worth having as a friend, that I have some personal security amid the risks and uncertainties of life. Besides, my friend is a "law" for me; I am challenged to live up to the friendship, to measure up to him and to what he expects of me. Similarly, the risen Christ speaks to us by his presence in the community of faith.

While the presence of Christ is a continuous reality in our lives, it is in and through the symbolic actions of Christian sacrament that he speaks most explicitly his meaning for us and the consequent significance of our life today. Such a statement depends, of course, on the Christian belief that Christ is actively present in the sacraments, that in them he expresses himself through the Church which is his body. If this faith be true, the sacraments are a special situation where Christ speaks to the assembled Christians the reality of his risen life, and where Christians can actually encounter Christ personally.

Sacraments contain many elements of explicitly formulated guidance for Christian faith and life: prayers, exhortation, creeds, and Scripture itself. As a result, the sacramental actions (particularly the celebration of the Eucharist) can be and are meant to be the principle instrument for the continuing religious education of the Christian people. Unfortunately, the widespread lack of truly meaningful celebration of sacraments has prevented these actions from having the pedagogical impact they are meant to have. The directives of Vatican II's decree on the liturgy are aimed principally at remedying this situation.

Beyond the more or less explicit directives for life that the sacramental liturgies contain, lies the "word" that is spoken in the sacraments by the presence of Christ. Confronted in the sacraments by the presence of the risen Christ who gives himself to them in love so that they might live more deeply, Christians are challenged to respond to him by their own love and dedication. With subtle but far-reaching impact, Christ's presence is meant to clarify for them the ultimate meaning of themselves and of their lives.

Christian life, then, is meant to be response to the word of God, a word that is constituted by the interaction of life itself, of Scripture, of the faith and life of the Christian community, and of sacrament. Together, these four elements should speak to Christians, individually and as a community, the revelation from God which will give human life its deepest significance and which will guide men towards the achievement of their destiny.

CHAPTER FIVE

The Worship of Life

ONE OF THE PUZZLING things about the New Testament writings, when one begins to reflect upon them from the viewpoint of a contemporary Christian, is their apparent lack of stress on religious ritual. At a time when we are striving to revivify the liturgical life of the Church, when we are stressing the importance of the eucharistic action, it seems strange that the New Testament literature pays so little attention to this element of Christian life.

This seeming de-emphasis of religious ritual becomes even more striking when one recalls the religious antecedents of the Christians who formed the early Church and produced the New Testament writings. To a large extent, these early Christians were drawn from Judaism. For them the worship of God had entailed the observance of the highly developed and closely regulated liturgy which we find reflected in Old Testament books like Leviticus. In fact, for some time after the resurrection of Jesus and the inception of Christianity itself, the early Christians continued to participate in Jewish worship. Clearly, they cherished the importance of religious ritual and honored the obligation of paying public worship to God.

Why, then, do we find practically nothing in the New Testament books that speaks to us directly about the kind of ritual that would be proper to Christianity? There are clear indications of the celebration of the Eucharist and of initiation into the community through baptism, but even the early

Christians' eucharistic "breaking of bread" was a familial gathering rather than a ritualized liturgy.

The impression received from many passages in the New Testament books is that the whole of life is meant to be the worship of God and that formalized ritual worship is of relatively little importance. But before one could legitimately proceed to the conclusion that this was really the outlook of the early Church, that this is the teaching of the New Testament writers, he would have to examine much more closely the mentality expressed in the New Testament books.

There is no doubt that the early Christians did not confine the notion of "worship" to formalized religious actions. The whole of Jesus' life and public ministry is worship of his Father, aimed at leading others to this worship. Paul's letters repeatedly exhort his hearers to worship the Father through the dedication of their entire life: "whether you eat or drink, or whatever you do, do all to the glory of God" (1 Cor. 10:31).

What kind of conclusion should one draw from such teaching? Are these writers really looking at the whole of life as worship in the formal sense, or is this a rhetorical way of stressing the basic dedication that should characterize a Christian's existence? If it means worship in the full sense, is it meant to replace religious ritual, as that is ordinarily understood, or is it meant to be a complementary expression of worship?

These questions, which the New Testament texts raise for us, find a strange coincidence with the questions being raised in our own day by many Christians who wonder about the need and effectiveness of formal religious practice. Many idealistic and dedicated men and women in our world, who know about Christianity but do not become Christians, do not see the need for formalized religion. More disturbing, considerable numbers of well-educated and sincere Christians are doubting the necessity and role of liturgical worship. Is it not much more important, they ask, to live one's life with integrity and concern for others, than to participate in worship actions that seem to have little impact on our world?

Worship in the Old Testament

Even earlier than the New Testament writings, the prophetic traditions of Old Testament Israel seem to be saying much the same thing as these modern voices. As far back as Hosea and Amos, one can find passages that seem to be anti-ritualistic: "I hate, I despise your feasts, and I take no delight in your solemn assemblies" (Amos 5:21). "I desire steadfast love and not sacrifice, the knowledge of God, rather than burnt offerings" (Hos. 6:6). One can, quite legitimately, point out that such sayings must be taken in the context of the prophets' total message; and that in this larger context the prophet is not truly advocating the abandonment of liturgical ritual, but giving strong rhetorical expression to the need to make this ritual an authentic act of worship.

But the prophetic oracles leave no doubt; in some basic fashion the entire fabric of Israel's life constituted the worship that Yahweh desired from his people. Sadly — and this was the accusation leveled by the prophets — this kind of worship was not forthcoming. In its absence, the liturgical celebrations were not an acceptable substitute. The faith of Israel, as it found expression in its most authentic spokesmen, the prophets, could not admit the validity of magical religion. Either religious ritual "came from the heart" or it was meaningless.

The position taken by the prophets in Israel seems eminently logical. Worship, after all, is the acknowledgement of God as he is. To direct some kind of "worship" to a divinity other than God as he reveals himself is idolatry, a violation of the first and most basic precept in Israel's law (Ex. 20:3). If this acknowledgement is to be genuine, it must be much more than a verbalized or dramatized statement; it must be the response of a people's entire life.

If Israel's faith-insight into the reality of God was essentially true, Yahweh was present to every step in Israel's development as a people, and present to each moment of an individual Israelite's life-experience. He was a merciful and saving divinity, who watched over his chosen ones, guiding

and protecting them, so that they could in free response to
him achieve their destiny. To acknowledge him as he thus revealed himself to them, meant that the people of the Old Testament had to accept this identity of a "saved people." They
had to live with trust in Yahweh, and depend upon him
rather than upon temporal power.

We know from the pages of the Old Testament that this
was exactly what the people were often reluctant to do. Their
leadership, in particular, tended to trust in its own devices:
the kings in their military and economic strength, the wise
men in their own understanding and cleverness, the priesthood in its ritual institutions. We cannot pass easy judgment
against this failing, for it is one that supposedly believing
Christians, at every level in the life of the Church, share with
Old Testament Israel. We, too, are unconscious to a large extent of our need for salvation, and mistakenly suppose that
we are capable of working out our destiny by our own efforts.
To the degree that Israel, or Christianity in its turn, has failed
to acknowledge its continuing dependence upon the loving
guidance of God, it has failed to worship the true God.

Jesus and Worship

Against this background of Old Testament prophetic
teaching, the Gospel description of the public ministry of
Jesus takes on deepened meaning. Jesus begins his public life
with the action of accepting baptism from John the Baptist,
which, as the Synoptics describe it, is a symbolic manifestation of his decision to undertake the role that is meant to be
his as the Servant-Messiah of Israel (Mt. 3:13-17). What,
exactly, this will entail is not yet evident in the scene of the
baptism; perhaps it was not known in its details by Jesus himself at that point in his human career. But the attitude of
Jesus that is expressed at that moment is clearly one of unre-
stricted commitment to the historical task that lies ahead of
him.

It is important to note, too, that the Gospel accounts indicate that this moment of publicly-manifested decision is one

involving Jesus' awareness of his relationship to the Father. The voice of the Father is heard (apparently, according to the accounts, only by Jesus himself): "This is my beloved Son, with whom I am well pleased" (Mt. 3:17). Here is a distinct advance beyond the Old Testament level of response to God. Jesus' acknowledgement of God retains all of the elements of Israel's understanding of and response to Yahweh, the god of the covenant whose care for his people could be metaphorically compared to a father's concern for his children, but it goes significantly beyond that. Jesus responds to one whom he knows to be, in a proper sense, his Father.

Immediately complementing the scene of the baptism at the Jordan is the scene of Jesus' temptation (Mt. 4:1-11). Here the nature of Jesus' baptismal acknowledgement of his Father is clarified by presenting in summary fashion the implications of the decision he has made. Three "temptations" that had confronted Old Testament Israel in its history — and to which Israel's response had been inadequate — are now presented to the Messiah: a magical approach, dependence upon wealth and power, a presumptuous demand that God protect man from a foolish course of action. To all three, Jesus' answer is clear and uncompromising. His final response, one that made the early Church realize a matter of worship was involved, is: "You shall worship the Lord your God and him only shall you serve" (Mt. 4:10).

The accounts of the baptism and temptation describe Jesus, then, as having repudiated alternatives to his Father's will for the establishment of the kingdom, as having rejected other suggested means of achieving human salvation. As Luke's Gospel tells us: Having refused earthly power and glory as the instruments he would employ to carry out his task, Jesus left the desert "in the power of the Spirit" (Lk. 4:14). Christ's public life, as portrayed for us by the Gospel traditions, is initiated by a public acceptance of the Father's wisdom and fidelity, that is, by an act of worship.

This event has many implications. We can note only those that touch upon our present study of the nature of Christian worship. In this regard, it is of fundamental importance that Jesus' action was one of straightforward acceptance of his own life-situation, his own specific role in human history. Obviously, the role in question — to be the Messiah of Israel and the savior of mankind — was a unique one. But this should not obscure the fact that Jesus of Nazareth, like any other man, did have a definite life-situation, a concrete set of circumstances, that formed the context of his decision.

Utilizing the insight provided by the scene of baptism-temptation, we can see how the entire public ministry of Jesus constitutes a continuing act of worship. Though the temptations of the desert come back in different forms throughout his public life, Jesus consistently rejects them. Though his witness to the truth his Father has sent him to communicate is met with opposition and increasingly dangerous hostility, he continues to preach the kingdom of his Father. The Jewish leadership, his own family, his closest disciples, all try to convince him that it is foolish to rely on this "unrealistic" approach, an approach that seems even more unrealistic as Jesus begins to declare explicitly that he must go to Jerusalem in order to suffer and die.

This unbending adherence to the mysterious plan of his Father for saving man seems to have been grounded in Jesus' trusting acceptance of his Father's love. While we can do little more than guess at the psychological reality that was Jesus' consciousness of his Father, it is evident that Jesus exhibited an unqualified openness to his Father. The final test of this complete acceptance of himself and his life-task in relation to the Father came with the threat of suffering and death. It was in death, freely accepted so that the Father's work of saving men might be accomplished, that Jesus gave his supreme testimony to his Father. This was the supreme moment of human worship.

This worshipful attitude of Jesus had several aspects. First of all, his acceptance of his life as a gift from his Father was not a once-for-all decision that took place on some occasion like the baptism. It was an acceptance that had to be constantly reiterated as the actual happenings of his life un-

folded. As the opposition from the leaders of the Jewish people mounted, as the crowds that earlier had flocked to him
began to drift away, Jesus had to decide in specific terms how
to carry out his prophetic and messianic task. It was the en-
tirety of this developing decision that made up his acknowledgement of the Father, an acknowledgement that was con-
cretized by the actual happenings of his life and death.

Again, the worship that Jesus directed toward his Father
was eminently personal. In him, all the psychological powers
of response that we associate with being humanly personal
— imagination, intellect, affectivity, emotions — were turned
in complete response to this other person, his Father, who
was supremely important to him. Worship of the Father was
for Jesus identical with love of his Father. His whole being as
man was an act of devoted dedication to the Father whom he
loved.

As a man, Jesus necessarily gave expression to his inner attitude to the Father, but it was the inner attitude that constituted the essence of his worship. His attitude was the realization of the ideal to which the prophets of Israel pointed, the
ideal that was finally crystallized in the figure of the Servant
contained in the second part of the book of Isaiah (Is. 52:53).
There are good indications in the Gospel texts that Jesus
claimed this title of "Servant" for himself, and used it to
characterize the work in which he was engaged. "The Son of
man came not to be served but to serve, and to give his life as
a ransom for many" (Mt. 20:28).

From the New Testament presentation of Jesus, of his life
and ministry and death, the Christian community can ascertain the kind of response it is meant to give the Father who
reveals himself in Jesus. While it may be necessary to have
some ritualized formulation of worship — a question we will
have to discuss later — it seems that the substance of Christian worship must consist in acknowledging the Father by an
honest acceptance of life. As a community and as individuals,
Christians must confront life as it is given to them in their
historical circumstances. To refuse the dictates of these circumstances, to resent their own identity and life-situation, is

subtly to repudiate the providential wisdom of God, to deny him as Father.

Life as Worship

An honest acceptance of reality is not just an acceptance of life; it is an acceptance of life lived in dependence. It is an admission of the human need for salvation. Men resist this admission. Involved in the human capacity for sin is the tendency to self-idolatry, the desire to be completely independent in fashioning one's own life, admitting no ultimate need for others, not even God. Examination of this attitude reveals it to be a self-destructive illusion, for it is impossible to attain even basic human selfhood except in relationship to and dependence upon others. Part of the mystery of sin is that men never thoroughly purge themselves of the illusion of complete independence.

Christian worship is meant to counter this illusion. It is meant to be not only a verbal admission of dependence upon a saving God, but a lived-out reliance upon the Father whose redeeming love comes to us in Jesus' life and death and resurrection. This is the approach to life that is constantly presented by the New Testament literature.

Paul's letters, particularly in their moral exhortations to the early Christian Churches, explicitly develop this view of life as worship. Writing to the Roman Church, Paul reminds them that both Jew and Gentile have hope of salvation only because of the merciful saving action of God. The response which he constantly urges upon them is that of living out the implications of God's graciousness to them. This response he sees as a dedication of self, which constitutes a basic act of worship: ". . . present your bodies as a living sacrifice, holy and acceptable to God, which is your spiritual worship" (Rom. 12:1).

With this perspective as a starting point, the next few chapters of Romans detail the outlook and behavior that comprise this "spiritual worship." The ideal of Christian life sketched by Paul is lofty, especially in its exhortation to respect the honest conscience-judgments of others, even if these conflict with one's own decisions. At the same time, Paul's directives deal with the down-to-earth matters that make up people's daily life, even the attitude the Christians should have toward the paying of taxes. Throughout, he urges a sensible and mature confrontation with life as it actually is, above all with people as they are, and an acceptance of that life with trust and hope in God.

Different members of the community will have different talents and gifts. Each one should utilize the gifts that are his, not envying the position or endowments of others, but fulfilling the role that he is meant to play in the community's life. By such cooperation and complementarity, the entire community becomes one "body of Christ," a truly unified and effective group of believers.

More important than the particular task a given individual performs is the spirit, the attitude, with which he performs it. This is true, even if there is question of some wishing to undertake some special religious practice. "He . . . who eats, eats in honor of the Lord, since he gives thanks to God; while he who abstains, abstains in honor of the Lord and gives thanks to God" (Rom. 14:6).

Above all, Christians must learn to live with people as they are, respecting their fundamental human dignity at the same time that they are aware of the limitations and frailty of human beings. Harmony and peace in human society, whether it be in the Christian community itself or in the wider context of mankind, can only be achieved if men and women are realistically and patiently willing to accept themselves and others, if they are genuinely concerned for one another rather than willing to exploit one another. In so honoring the dignity of their fellow-men, and thus furthering concord among men, Christians will honor mankind's common Father (Rom. 12-15).

Worship and Social Justice

Paul's emphasis on the Christians' need to foster reverential attitudes towards their fellow-human beings brings us into contact with a biblical theme that we must examine more carefully, if we are to understand the mentality of Scripture regarding worship. This theme, related to the one we have just been discussing, is the inseparable connection between worship of God and social justice. Respect for the dignity and rights of all men is but a part of the attitude of forthright acceptance of reality as it comes from the creative providence of God. It is such an important part and is so constantly emphasized by the biblical literature, that it merits special attention.

By way of introduction, one could say — and we will then have to look at the texts of the Bible to substantiate the statement — that worship of the God who reveals himself in Old Testament times and in Jesus is inseparable from, even partially identical with, social justice and charity. Unless a man acknowledges all other men and women as his brothers and sisters, and expresses this practically in the manner in which he deals with them, he cannot truthfully acknowledge this God as he is: the heavenly Father of all humankind.

The social concern of Israel's great prophets and their resounding condemnation of the oppression and injustice of their day is too obvious and well known to require any extensive treatment here. What we wish to emphasize is the link they see between this social situation and the cultic practice of the chosen people.

At first glance, some of the prophets, like Amos and Jeremiah, seem hostile to religious ritual. Their condemnatory rhetoric is so strong, that they seem to be saying to the Israelites of their day, "forget about your worship at the shrines." But what they are saying, when one examines the texts more closely, is: "Unless you stop the exploitation of the poor, unless you are willing to honor the needs and rights of your fellow-men, your ritual acts of worship are meaningless and hypocritical."

The legitimacy of this connection between authentic worship and social concern is apparent. The God who reveals himself to the Old Testament people is, even according to their fairly primitive religious understanding, a "spiritual" divinity. That is, he himself has no physical need of, nor can he derive any physical enjoyment from, the sacrificial gifts that the Israelites bring to him in their religious rituals. If these gifts serve any authentic purpose as part of an act of worship, it is only because they are functioning symbolically to give expression to the interior attitude of the worshipping community. They are a sign, a "word," in which the people respond to Yahweh's own word of revelation, in which they accept in faith his reality as he has revealed it.

But, say the prophets, if the worshipping Israelites speak this word of ritual when their attitude towards their fellowman is not one of justice and concern, the word of ritual is a lie. As such, it is a flagrant affront to the God they are pretending to worship; either it denies that he is the kind of God he has revealed himself to be — a God who is interested in saving all men — or it presumes that he is ignorant of their malice and effectively deceived by their external show of devotion.

Seen in this light, the liturgical ceremonial of Israel is not true worship as long as the people refuse to right the social wrongs of their day. Such worship comes much closer to blasphemy or idolatry. The prophetic oracles of condemnation often couple the two accusations of injustice and idolatry. At times the prophets might seem to be identifying the two charges. This is too facile a judgment, because the prophets were also pointing to the more obvious and crass forms of idolatry that involved the people in some of the religious rites of the neighboring cultures. However, it does seem that the prophets saw a strong and intrinsic link between those two major sins of their people.

One can approach the situation from a slightly different point of view and arrive at the same conclusion: Throughout the liturgical history of Old Testament Israel, worship was closely associated with the law. Proclamation of the law and explanation of it seems to have formed not only a preparatory introduction to the act of worship, but, on many occasions at least, a regular portion of the liturgical action. This means that the entire act of worship was, at least implicitly, an acceptance of this law and a pledge to observe it.

It would have been a travesty of worship if, as the prophets say in accusation, the people ritually professed their adherence to this law and then proceeded to ignore its prescriptions regulating their social existence. Israel's characteristic understanding of law was that all the law governing their life was the expression of the will of Yahweh; there was no law that was sheerly civil or secular. Worship as an act of commitment to Yahweh's will was radically incompatible with a regular and stubborn violation of the rights of men which the laws were meant to guarantee.

New Testament teaching builds upon, absorbs, and goes beyond the prophets' position. Jesus is described as linking explicitly the act of worship with relationship to one's fellowman: "So if you are offering your gift at the altar, and there remember that your brother has something against you, leave your gift there before the altar and go; first be reconciled to your brother, and then come and offer your gift" (Mt. 5:23).

Like the prophets before him, Jesus in his public teaching attacks the social injustices and exploitation of his day, in which, tragically, some of the religious leadership itself was involved. Even the Jerusalem Temple precincts seem to have been used by money changers who defrauded the poor and simple people. Against such a perversion of the Temple's role, the wrath of Jesus reacted in the scene of the cleansing of the Temple, his first act after he entered the city on Palm Sunday to begin the formal stage of establishing his Father's kingdom.

One of the most instructive passages in the New Testament literature is the parable of the good Samaritan (Lk. 10:33). It is possible to read this parable and see in it nothing more than a judgment against those who are too busy about their own affairs to care for those in need. On the other hand, it seems that the intent of the parable is more specific. For the priest and the Levite who passed by the robbed and beaten man there was a "conflict" between the human demand to

take care of the suffering man and the ritual regulations of
their official liturgical position — to have cared for the beaten
and bloodied man would have made them unclean for their
ritual task.

The lesson of the parable viewed in this light is obvious. In
such a situation of human need, the operative law was that of
providing for this need. The two liturgical functionaries were
not justified in preserving the ceremonial law at the expense
of neglecting a fellow-human in distress. What could their ritual activity mean except an empty fulfillment of rubrical prescriptions, abstracted from life and reality? Interestingly, the
parable says that it was a Samaritan — by Jewish standards a
man incapable of giving divinely-recognized liturgical worship
to God — who gave true praise to God by his action of
mercy. It was a Samaritan, rather than two members of Judaism's special religious caste, who understood the words of
Hosea, "I desire steadfast love and not sacrifice" (Hos. 6:6).

Again, a study of the parable of the last judgment in Matthew's Gospel (Mt. 25:31) reveals a profound link between
worship and social concern. According to this teaching,
which Matthew places as the final parable of Jesus, the evaluation of a man's life will be made on the basis of his care for
the hungry, the thirsty, those in any other situation of need.
What is specially interesting from the point of view of what
constitutes worship is the statement that care for the needy
involves a recognition of God, even though in some cases the
recognition is only implicit. "Whatsoever you did to the least
of my brethren, you did to me."

The most profound instance of the link between worship
and concern for one's fellow-men comes in Jesus' own attitude and behavior. Throughout his life, but most specially in
his death and resurrection, his acknowledgement of his Father and his dedication to the redemption of men coalesce
into one attitude, for his Father's will is the redemption of
men. This intention is shown clearly in the action of the Last
Supper. This act of covenant worship of his Father consists
precisely in the symbolic act of giving himself to his disciples.

If Jesus' human acknowledgement of his Father consisted in an uncompromising acceptance of his own human life-situation, as we said earlier, then he saw and accepted his relationship to other men as the very heart of that life-situation.

There seems no doubt about the link between life and worship in the biblical perspective. Whatever meaning worship has, it must be in some fashion linked with the intrinsic meaning and responsibilities of the life of those who worship. Unless life be maturely faced and its demands honestly assessed, worship is at best meaningless and at worst a lie.

This brings us to the second major portion of our study of worship. If man's basic response to life is so intrinsic to the validity of the religious ritual, why does this response not suffice? Why must there be the externalization of man's fundamental acknowledgement of God, since God surely does not need such a formalized expression?

Worship as Symbol

In attempting some answer to this question, and more specifically in searching the New Testament writings for some guidelines to an answer, one must look carefully at the symbolic actions that are attributed to Jesus in the Gospels. We have already mentioned the lack of attention to Jesus' performance of the Jewish liturgical ritual. Unquestionably, he did share in the Jewish worship ceremonial, as did any devout Jew of his day, but the Gospel writers apparently see little significance in this. What is emphasized instead is the symbolic aspect of Jesus' actions of healing. These are his "signs," which prepare for an understanding of the greatest of them, his death and resurrection.

Three happenings in Jesus' public life seem to be given particular prominence: his baptism at the Jordan, the transfiguration, and the Last Supper. All three are described with conscious reference to their many-layered symbolism, and two of them at least — the baptism and the supper — are closely linked with the early Christian practice of what we now identify as sacramental ritual.

Before going on to a study of these key New Testament passages, it might be well to recall briefly the role that symbols play both in man's individual life and in the shared life of men in community. Modern philosophers have paid great attention to the function of symbols in man's consciousness and activity. Some have seen this function as the most characteristic element of man's way of existing — man is a symbol-making being. While this interest in human use of symbol may be more intense today, it is not entirely new. For many centuries there has been lengthy, and sometimes heated, discussion about the relation of human consciousness to its symbolic expression in language. However, there is relatively more attention paid today to man's inner state of consciousness. The development of psychological research and formalized psychological therapy is a clear indication of this interest, which has led to many interesting insights into the impact of symbols on human consciousness.

As far back as we have any record of man, there has always been the attempt to find some meaning in human existence, and men have always tried to express the meaning they did "discover." These expressions, in myths or legends or artistic creations or religious ritual, were attempts to state in compressed and explicit fashion the significance of everything else that men were, or did, or suffered. Once formulated, such symbolic realities had a strong influence on the way in which people understood their lives. On the other hand, the life-experience of people constantly injected new elements of meaning into these symbols. The development of symbols within a given culture thus provides us with a valuable index to the evolution of that culture.

Our own age is no different, though the precise symbolic forms we use may be different. We still employ certain sensible actions or things — dance, sculpture, movies, flags — to give expression to the meaning we find (or do not find) in our life. It is not as though we have clearly in mind the significance of life today, and then proceed to find apt media for expressing it. Often enough, probably most often, we are vague about the meaning we do find in life and the very process of using some symbols is part of our attempt to discover meaning. In the painting of a picture, or the writing of a poem, or the making of a film, the artist discovers what it is that he is trying to say; the symbol produced serves to clarify the consciousness of its creator as well as the consciousness of others to whom it might be addressed.

Nor must we suppose that this process is limited only to those situations of artistic expression, where the density of the symbolism is more apparent. The same psychological reality is verified in something as ordinary as a college student writing a term paper. Most people — college students are only an example — resist the process of expressing their ideas in written form. To some extent this may be due to a lack of facility in writing, but for most of us it is also due to the fact that our ideas are not as clear as we think they are; we do not know exactly what we want to say. When we are forced to write, the very task of expressing ourselves in the symbols of the language makes us clarify our understandings.

Using symbols, then, seems to be not only helpful but even necessary for us, if we wish to develop our life of consciousness. This need becomes even more evident when one realizes how interdependent we humans are for the development of our intellectual and personal lives. Education, which is essential to our growth and maturation, obviously depends upon the whole system of symbols that we use in communicating with one another. Human society, in its various forms, would be impossible if there were not such symbolic realities like language, by which a community of understanding and purpose can be achieved.

Language is the most apparent and most pervasive kind of symbol that works to knit human society together. There are other less apparent, but very powerful, symbols that help to effect the similarity of consciousness and attitude that is required for human community. Again, modern psychological and anthropological studies have done much to draw our attention to these key cultural symbols, and to clarify the manner in which these symbols work in the "corporate psyche" of a group of people.

Let us take just one homely and perhaps not too important example. Each November, throughout the United States, families celebrate Thanksgiving Day. The dinner that day is not just another meal; it has some special meaning, even though most people do not dwell much on its precise significance. A prominent aspect of its significance is indicated by the very name of the day, a day which is an occasion for the entire nation to express its gratitude to God for the blessings enjoyed by our people. There is in addition — and this is what touches on our present discussion of community symbol — a recollection of the Pilgrim Fathers, of the early origins of our country. No matter how little attention is paid today to the actual happenings of early American history, or to the lives and fortunes of those early colonists, there is probably no group in the United States that celebrates Thanksgiving Day without some vague recollection of the Pilgrims.

Because of this, Thanksgiving Day serves to create and preserve an element of our common identification. We share with one another this historical heritage, which includes our colonial origins. We share also a certain national pride, and a willing acceptance of our situation as citizens of this country; otherwise we would not be celebrating our gratitude.

As we said, this particular example does not take us too deeply into the social psychology of the American people, but even such simple "folk liturgy" does have its impact on the manner in which a given group sees the significance of its life. After all, it was from such celebrations in the ancient world, though many of them were meant to be more explicitly religious liturgies, that our use of a calendar originated. And the calendar is one of the means we use to make our existence in time more intelligible.

Symbols that people share not only convey some common understanding, they also express and reinforce attitudes and value-judgments. In this regard, the effects of television, especially the techniques of advertizing in television commercials, provide a fascinating study. Anyone who views television for even a short time must become aware that one of the great symbols operating in the American consciousness is that of "youth." Youth, with its vitality and energy, with its carefree enjoyment of life, is constantly presented as the ideal period of human existence. This symbol is then used to sell everything from soft drinks to automobiles to toothpaste, the implication in the commercials being that somehow one will share in the ideal of youth by buying such products.

There are innumerable other elements of our American way of life that symbolize the values we cherish: the automobiles we drive, the kinds of social clubs we form, the neglect of our inner cities and of the people who must live there, the money we pay our famous and popular athletes, our universities and research centers, our concert halls and art museums, our churches and our cocktail lounges. Not only do these mirror the value-judgments we constantly make, they form the environment in which all of us are acquiring and adjusting our personal evaluation of life and of what is worth seeking from life.

Inseparably linked with the impact that symbols have on man's view of life and on the values man possesses, is the role of symbols in human decision-making. From what we have already seen, it is clear that symbols play a large part in the development of understanding and evaluation, which lead to decision. But symbols are operative, too, in the very act of deciding.

Signing of contracts, marriage ceremonies, promulgation of laws, political elections — all these are indications of the fact that we constantly and necessarily express our decisions, so that social life based on these decisions can be carried on with assurance and clarity. The performance of the symbolic action forms an intrinsic part of the decision. We do not hold a person to responsibility for the decision until this external element is present.

Psychologically, we all experience the fact that externalizing our decisions by some sign enters into the process of deciding. Often, we think that we have decided some matter, but then discover how indecisive we still are when we are asked to state our choice. Once we give expression to a decision, by speaking or by some other symbolic action, we are committed to it; it must really function as a decision and not only as a wish or an inclination. On occasion, it is only in expressing a decision that we realize just what it is that we are deciding. For these very reasons, many people are hesitant about giving expression to a decision. More exactly, they are hesitant about making decisions.

Christian Sacraments

We see, then, that symbols of various kinds pervade the entire fabric of our human experience, giving meaning and shape and direction to that experience. Christian sacraments are meant to be a key aspect of such symbolic influence, providing the specific significance and impact that derives from the reality of Jesus' life and death and resurrection. The insights and values connected with Christian sacraments, since they touch upon all the fundamental experiences of life — birth, suffering, joy, love, decision, sexuality, death, community — should interrelate with all the other symbolisms that function in human consciousness.

We can grasp some of the symbolic power inherent in Christian sacraments, if we reflect on the fact that the meaning of Jesus' death is meant to be infused into human experience by each of the sacraments. No other element of human life is more profoundly significant than death; no other element has greater impact on the entire experience of man. Life itself takes on different meanings for individuals and cultures dependent on their understanding of and emotional response to death. In his own death, Jesus of Nazareth transformed radically the meaning of death, making it the entry into unending life. It is this meaning that Christian sacraments are meant to convey to man's understanding, thus transforming his view of life itself.

In similar fashion, all the other elements of Jesus' human life and resurrection are meant to shed light on the intrinsic meaning of the human situation. By becoming man and himself experiencing the whole range of events that comprise the basic life-experience of humans, Jesus infused his own meaning into life. Thereby, he laid the ground for Christian sacraments, which are meant to convey that meaning to the lives of men and women in each generation.

As the Gospels describe him for us, Jesus is the fulfillment of the wisdom movement of the Old Testament. Not only is he the greatest teacher of wisdom, he is the very embodiment of the wisdom that God conveys to men (Mt. 11). With him a new level of values enters into human life and judgment. It is these values that Christian sacraments are intended to transmit to Christians and through them to the lives of all men.

Exposed in sacrament to the reality of the risen Christ, to the mystery of his death and resurrection into which he entered because of his love for men and his desire to share life with them, Christians should evaluate with added depth the good and evil that touches their lives. This set of values will not be opposed to the authentic values that other men and women espouse, nor does Christianity alone claim to follow an exalted set of values, but the very existence of the risen Christ and his influence on men for their salvation introduces a new and more ultimate value into man's experience. Other religions or cultures can, and in some instances do, share with the New Testament writings the judgment that human persons are always of more importance than things, that men should never be subordinated to things or to institutions; but in Christianity this judgment is grounded in Christ's own relationship to and concern for each human person.

Such values are expressed explicitly in the liturgical ceremonies of Christian sacraments, especially in the use of Scripture during the eucharistic action. However, the deepest impact on Christians' value-judgments is meant to come through the profoundly symbolic act of the risen Christ giving himself bodily to men through the signs of bread and wine. This experience of the risen Lord giving himself personally to them should cause in the Christians who celebrate the Eucharist an insight into their own great personal worth and the personal worth of all other men and women.

Finally — and again we can do little more at this point than suggest the topic — the Christian sacraments are quite clearly meant to be symbolic actions that give expression to the decision of the people who perform the action. Baptism and confirmation state the person's choice to share in the life of the Christian community; marriage and priestly ordination commit persons to a particular role within the community; penance and anointing signify the decision of people to strive faithfully to fulfill their Christian identity despite the evils that afflict humans; and the Eucharist, precisely because it is a continuing act of covenant, expresses the community's determination to live out in daily existence the implications of Christ's death and resurrection.

Though such sacramental actions have often tended to become, at least in the view of the Christians who performed them, special "religious" actions, apart from the rest of their lives, this should not be the case. The significance of Christian sacraments includes the entire context of meanings and values and decisions that enter into the lives of Christians. For this reason, sacraments cannot be authentically celebrated by a Christian community without a basic commitment to life as a whole. They are meant to be the formal, ritual expression of the grateful and responsible acceptance of life that constitutes the Christian community's worship of God the Father.

Baptism, Transfiguration, the Last Supper

This conjunction of life and ritual-symbols to form one continuing act of worship is clearly exemplified in the career of Jesus as it is presented by the Gospels. Three key passages — the baptism at the Jordan, the transfiguration, and the Last Supper — are specially interesting and revealing in this regard. Each of these involves two elements, one clearly symbolic and the other expressing the same meaning in more "ordinary" fashion. The baptism is followed immediately by the temptation, the transfiguration is linked with the prediction of the passion, the Supper is linked with the agony in the garden. These three passages, more than any others, serve as principles of understanding for the entire Gospel.

Comparative study of the parallel Gospel accounts of these three events indicates a rich and fascinating complementarity of theological insight on the part of the four evangelists. For simplicity's sake we might follow here the text of Luke's Gospel (Lk. 3; 9:28-36; 22:14-38). For one thing, as we will see, it is he who most explicitly places these events in a context of worship.

Jesus' baptism by John at the Jordan is obviously a symbolic action. Like the others who accepted baptism by John, Jesus indicated his acceptance of John's prophetic message. John was proclaiming the early advent of the kingdom of God and the need for conversion. Those baptized by him were thus giving symbolic expression to their acceptance of John's message and their willingness to share in the establishment of the kingdom of God about which he spoke. Jesus' willingness to be baptized by John was a public testimony to his choice to work for this kingdom that "was at hand."

In Jesus' case, however, the role to which he was called in the task of establishing the kingdom was unique, as the Gospel traditions indicate in the scene at the Jordan. Jesus is seen to be the new Israel who recapitulates in his own life-experience the Old Testament event of the Exodus. He is the Messiah, according to the insights contained in the "servant songs" of Deutero-Isaiah. He also seems to be seen, in Luke's perspective, as the new Adam. No matter how much, or how little, conscious theological reflection one wishes to attribute to the various evangelists as they narrate the baptism scene, it is clear that the Gospels' description of the baptism at the Jordan is deeply symbolic.

It is also clear that the baptism was a moment of both decision and insight for Jesus. In saying this, we are, of course, dealing with the event as described by the Gospel writers; we have no way of knowing exactly what Jesus experienced as he began his public ministry. The Gospel writers are much more interested in pointing to the significance of the baptism than they are in giving a detailed factual report, which means that the evangelists are chiefly interested in the symbolic dimensions of these scenes.

Thus, though we do not know exactly how Jesus envisaged the public ministry upon which he entered with his baptism, it is clear that he does undertake that ministry at this point. Later developments in his prophetic career seem to indicate that Jesus began his work faced with obscurity about the future, just as all men do. What he is described as doing at the Jordan is committing himself to the messianic role of working to establish the kingdom of his Father, and doing so with reliance upon the Father. His decision is a covenant decision, related to the decision that was asked of Israel throughout the centuries of Old Testament history.

As a wholehearted covenant decision, Jesus' act was acknowledgement of his Father and an act of worship. As described in the Gospels, this was also for Jesus a moment of deepened insight. In the very act of accepting his life and its demands from his Father, Jesus received from his Father, in his human knowing, a deepened vision of his own identity and task. The voice from heaven speaks to Jesus, "Thou art my beloved Son; with thee I am well pleased" (Lk. 3:22). Again, we are at a loss to know precisely what this experience was for Jesus, how it added to his understanding of himself and of his prophetic mission. The Gospel traditions apparently agree that only Jesus heard the words of the Father; this would mean that they considered the moment in Jesus' experience as one of new, or at least deepened, insight. His "call" at the Jordan is reminiscent of the Old Testament passages which describe the initial vocation-experience of the great charismatic prophets (cf. Jer. 1).

Densely symbolic in nature, the scene of the baptism is

immediately complemented in the Gospel narratives by the scene of Jesus' temptation in the desert. It is the series of temptations that Jesus is there described as undergoing that spells out the implications of the choice he had symbolically expressed in the baptism. As with the baptism, it is impossible to ascertain exactly what happened to Jesus at this point: whether the temptations occurred as described, whether the actuality of the temptations took place entirely within the consciousness and imagination of Jesus (which, incidentally, would not make them less "real"), or whether the description as we have it in the texts is a graphic way of summarizing the temptations that came to Jesus in the course of his ministry. Again, as with the baptism, the answer to the question is irrelevant to the issue we are studying. The scene of the temptation is intended to indicate the issues of choice contained symbolically in the baptism and thereafter expressed by Jesus in the actualities of his ministry and passion.

What is also shown by the texts is that the suggestions of "the tempter" are alternate choices as to how Jesus should carry out his proposed work of helping men, choices which would constitute an unwillingness to accept the realities of life as it faced him. The alternatives proposed to Jesus are clearly presented as those fundamental religious temptations that enter the decisions of all men; actually, in the text, they are presented as summarizing the key temptations of Old Testament Israel. By refusing these compromising alternatives, Jesus gives witness to his belief in the wisdom of his Father.

Intrinsically, the action of Jesus in the baptism and temptation constitutes an act of worship, an acknowledgement of his Father. In Luke's account, explicit attention is drawn to this act. In comparing Luke's text with those of the other two synoptic Gospels one notices that the short phrase is added, "as Jesus was praying." Jesus' attitude during the scene is explicitly described as one of worship, but it is this same attitude which is Jesus' act of choice. Since this act of choice runs throughout the public ministry of Jesus, being modified only insofar as it must come to grips with the changing demands of those months, we can see how the entire activity of Jesus can rightly be called an act of worship. It is, however, the symbolic scene of the baptism that clarifies the worship aspects of the public ministry.

We can notice the same complementarity of symbolic act and daily life when we examine the Gospel scene of the transfiguration and its relation to Jesus' prediction of his suffering and death (Lk. 9:28-45). In many ways, the scene of the transfiguration of Jesus is the turning point in the dramatic structure of Christ's public life. Shortly before occurs the multiplication of the loaves, which was a richly meaningful sign that Jesus had worked in the presence of several thousand, a sign whose meaning should have been grasped by the people in the light of Jesus' earlier teaching. But the true significance of the act was missed by the crowds (Jn. 6), many of whom began at this point to drift away from Jesus.

Even some of Jesus' closer disciples began to entertain some doubts, for it now seemed that Jesus was not to claim and win earthly kingship. All four Gospels relate, though in somewhat different form, that Jesus apparently found it necessary to question even the Twelve, to see if they also would leave him. It was at this point that Simon Peter, forced to face the issue of his own personal estimate of Jesus, came to the realization that Jesus was indeed Israel's Messiah. But the crucial question was: What kind of Messiah?

As the Gospels narrate it, the event of the transfiguration was a critical step in clarifying the unique manner in which Jesus was to fulfill the messianic expectations. Like the scene of the baptism, the transfiguration is described in highly symbolic fashion, with much of its symbolism reaching back, as did that of the baptism, into the history of Israel. It would be fascinating to probe the antecedents and implications of all those symbolic elements, but that would take us too far from our present objective. What is germane to our present discussion is the fact that all these symbolic implications indicate the profound significance of the decision taken by Jesus at this moment.

The decision was not fundamentally other than that already expressed at the baptism and temptation, nor was Jesus' fundamental understanding of his identity and role changed; the same words of the Father are here repeated, "This is my beloved son . . . ." But the decision is now made after the experience of mixed acceptance and rejection of his teaching. It is made in the light of the mounting opposition of the Jewish leadership. It is made after the murder of John the Baptist, which apparently affected Jesus deeply. The decision, as Luke specifies it, is that of Jesus undertaking his "exodus."

Luke again adds to the text, "as Jesus was praying," thus placing the transfiguration, as he had the baptism, in the formal context of worshipful recognition of the Father. There are other overtones of ritual worship which Luke shares with the other accounts, for some of the details of the scene are apparently meant to relate to the liturgy for the Jewish feast of Tabernacles. Once more, it is Jesus' act of decision that is his act of worship.

What is involved in this decision becomes immediately clear as Jesus talks to his disciples as they descend from the mountain. He must go down to Jerusalem, and there suffer and die. Such a decision is completely paradoxical as far as his disciples are concerned. Had they not just arrived at the insight that he was the Messiah? Certainly this was not a fitting way of carrying out his messianic role. Jesus refuses their suggestions, just as he had those of the tempter in the desert, and "sets his face for Jerusalem." Unswervingly he carries out his decision to preach a message of conversion to the Father, even though such a course of action promises to lead to death.

As with the baptism and temptation, we can see in the transfiguration and prediction of the passion the double expression, symbolic and "ordinary," of the one attitude and decision. In probing the rich symbolic connotations of the transfiguration, we can see the many elements of meaning that are involved in the decision Jesus made, the background of Jewish understanding that flowed into the decision, the role of the decision in the course of salvation history. But it is in the actual sequence of events following this symbolic act that we discover the translation into life and suffering and death of the decision. Neither element of this complementary "doublet" can be understood without the other.

More explicitly than either baptism or transfiguration, the Supper is described in the Gospels as an act of worship (Lk. 22:14-28). The entire context of Jesus' gathering with his disciples in the upper room is cultic, for it is a Paschal gathering. Scholars are still divided as to whether or not Jesus and his disciples actually ate the Passover meal that evening; there are some inconsistencies in the chronology of events as narrated in the different Gospels. But is is clear in all the Gospels that the Last Supper caught up into itself all the historical and cultic symbolisms of the Jewish Pasch and transformed them.

Jesus' action at the Supper is related to the covenant celebrations of Israel, even to the first enacting of the Sinai covenant as it is described in Exodus 24. An expression like "my blood which is poured out for you" (which Jesus uses of the cup of wine at the Supper) seems connected in the Gospel writers' thoughts to the ritual use of blood in the sacrifices of Old Testament Israel. In the text of Luke, we do not find the phrase "as Jesus was praying," which was used for the baptism and transfiguration to indicate Jesus' attitude of worship; instead, the word *eucharistesas* (giving thanks) is used as a more precise designation of the prayer of Jesus at the Supper.

The Supper, then, is explicitly described as an act of ritual worship. At the same time, it is the occasion for Jesus' most solemn and definitive statement of his lifelong decision to fulfill his Father's will. That will had been, and was, that he, Jesus, give himself to men for their salvation, even to the point of death. At the Supper, in the first stage of the action which will then carry on into his death and resurrection, Jesus gives himself to his disciples through the symbolic sharing of the bread and wine.

Christian faith and theology have always stated that Jesus

in his suffering and death was a victim offered for the salvation of men. The texts of the New Testament support this view, especially in the way in which they relate Jesus to the figure of the suffering servant (described in Isaiah 52-53). However, it is important to note how clearly the New Testament writers indicate the key role of Jesus' own free choice. He is not a forced or unwilling victim; he himself chooses to give himself to his brethren for their redemption. If we probe more deeply into the reality of his victimhood, into the fact that he is "placed aside" as solemnly dedicated to the sacred purpose of achieving salvation, we see that the reality which constitutes him as a victim is his own act of decision.

All this is indicated in the scene of the Supper. It is an action of covenant, an action in which God through Jesus freely but irrevocably binds himself to men, and in which mankind in Jesus is irrevocably committed to the service of the Father. As in all covenants, there is a solemn expression of the decision of both parties to the relationship being established. The unique element in the covenant action of the Supper is the convergence of these two decisions in Jesus himself. His decision and its manifestation through his symbolic giving of self to the disciples is sacramental of the Father's decision to save men. At the same time, as the representative of all mankind, Jesus, through his decision and its expression in the worship-act of the Supper, links all men to his Father.

If the scenes of the baptism and the transfiguration provided an insight into the significance of Jesus' actions of public ministry, the Supper is even more instructive. It is the Supper, whose symbolic richness is literally inexhaustible, that links our understanding with all the significance of human life and history. Most immediately, and this is probably what was primarily intended by the Gospel writers in describing it, the Supper points to the meaning of Jesus' death and resurrection. It is the Supper, the first stage in Jesus' passage into the new promised land of resurrection, that establishes the meaning of Christ's passion, death, and resurrection. It is the Supper, along with death and resurrection — from

which it is inseparable — that throws full light upon the earlier life and activity of Jesus.

Having pledged himself in the symbol of the Supper to give himself to men through death and resurrection, Jesus left the upper room to enter his passion. Just as the scene of the temptation and the prediction of his passion complemented the symbolic acts of baptism and transfiguration, the passion of Jesus, which begins in the garden of Gethsemane, gives realistic expression to the meaning of the Supper (Lk. 23:39-46). If the Supper was a solemn pledge by which Jesus gave himself to men, the actual death and resurrection of Jesus indicate what was involved in that pledge.

As the passion experience begins to unfold for Jesus in his prayerful agony in the garden, it seems that the full psychological impact of what he is doing descends upon him. Confronted with the immediate prospect of suffering and death, he recoils emotionally from the implications of the decision that is his. In the keen anguish of that moment, Jesus remains faithful to his decision, continues with his passion, and fulfills without compromise his destiny.

As the passion narratives describe it, the scene of the agony in the garden forms part of the same supreme act of choice that was begun in the upper room at the Supper. Like the Supper, the scene of the agony is a situation of worship. Faced with the enigmatic fact that his Father wished him to undergo the torment of passion and death, Jesus still retained his trust in the Father's love and bore witness to that trust by accepting the mysterious demands of his life-situation. Jesus' action in the garden is at once a prayer and the reiteration of a decision, an acknowledgement of his Father in terms of the concrete realities of human life and death. As such, it teaches us who are Christians the intrinsic nature of Christian worship.

Sacramental Worship

At this point, we can return to the question we raised at the beginning of the chapter: What, if any, purpose does ritualized worship play in the life of a Christian? Now we can say that such formal liturgical expression of worship serves a very definite purpose; that it is, in fact, indispensable. Grateful and responsible acceptance of life must always be the basic element of authentic Christian worship. Such acceptance demands externalization in religious ritual.

A truly Christian acceptance of life must be grounded in a continuing and evolving insight into the Christian meaning of life. The celebration of Christian sacraments explicitly draws attention to this Christ-meaning, and thereby makes it possible for Christians, as individuals and as a community, to inject this meaning into their daily experience. Not only do such sacramental worship-situations provide the context in which each Christian's understanding of Christ's death and resurrection can be clarified and brought into relationship with his own life experience; but is in such community profession of faith that Christians can share with one another their understanding of Christianity and thus form a true community of believers.

Confronted in sacramental ritual with the values of the Gospel, a Christian community can then communally espouse and share these values. Obviously, each of the Christians present must ultimately make his own personal decisions in this regard, but the support of the community is of considerable importance in making the demanding decision to live according to the Gospel. The challenge presented by the actions of the sacraments is not just that of the values that were taught and exemplified by Jesus; the ultimate challenge is the person of Jesus himself, the risen Lord, whom Christian faith sees as present and active in the sacraments. The challenge is that of responding to Christ's own gift of self in love, which is the ultimate value.

The challenge presented in the sacraments is spelled out in everyday life. Here the decision expressed by a Christian community in liturgical worship must find fulfillment. This day-by-day human existence constitutes the Christian people's response to the Father, but to the Father as he reveals himself in and through the risen Christ, made specially present through the "word" of sacramental action. The world to which Christians respond because they see it, too, as a form of word from God, is a world in which faith perceives the presence and activity of Christ and the Spirit. The sacraments are intended to keep Christians constantly alert to this deeper level of reality and meaning.

Perhaps the deepest reason for ritual worship of God through Christian sacrament is this: Ultimately, the only truly adequate and sufficient act of human worship is that of Christ himself. In sacrament, the Christian community unites the worship of its own life to that of the risen Christ. In this union, the acknowledgement of the Father by the assembled Christians attains a dignity and fullness it could not otherwise have. Christ's own acknowledgement of his Father finds its fulfillment in and through the Spirit. As Paul tells the early Christians, only in the Spirit are they able to speak the ultimate word of worship. "Abba, Father." This is what a Christian community, sharing the Spirit that Christ gives to them, is able to do in sacrament, above all in the greatest of the sacraments, the action of the Eucharist.

CHAPTER SIX

God, Hidden and Revealed

BENEATH ALL the other questions about religion that men have had or that they have today lies the basic query: Who or what is God, if there is a God? That this is not an artificial question is abundantly proved by the contemporary world of thought. Every religious group in the world is presently going through a critical appraisal of its understanding of the divine, in part because of the inescapable challenge of atheism and agnosticism, but also because of the maturing of religious thought itself.

Some analysts of the contemporary scene claim — and there is solid evidence to support the claim — that the modern age is characterized by a loss of the sense of God, a loss more radical and total than anything that men have experienced. Earlier ages had, of course, their atheists and their agnostics, but to some extent they were denying the God "who was there." Living in a culture that still accepted in some fashion, as a basically undisputed reality, the existence of the transcendent, these atheists of old denied explicitly the "god" they implicitly recognized in many aspects of their culture. For about a century, especially in the West, there has been a new phenomenon, the emergence of a culture that seems to be completely without reference to any transcendent.

The Challenge of Secularity

The kind of secularity that characterizes the lives and thought of most Americans, the Marxist materialism that finds expression in the Soviet Union, are but two examples of such "godless" human life in our world. What is involved is not the expressed denial of the divine by professed atheists, though there is always some of this, but the much further-reaching lack in many people's lives of any reference to a god. In increasing numbers men and women live their daily lives without any awareness whatsoever of the divine, and apparently without any awareness of such a need.

It is still too early to make a careful historical judgment about this modern secularism. Is it truly rejection, or even an attack upon God, or is it grounded in ignorance about man's deepest understandings of the divine? Is it merely a protest against grossly inadequate descriptions of God by men who claim to be religious? There are some indications that much of this so-called "secularity" may actually be deeply religious, that its roots may lie in certain aspects of Christianity itself.

One of the most intriguing and puzzling facts about the contemporary attitude towards the divine is this: Despite the widespread rejection of the divine by what we might call broadly "modern philosophy," despite the predominance of the kind of secularity we were just describing, our contemporary art-forms frequently raise the question of God. This preoccupation with the matter of man's ultimate frame of reference, of his destiny, of his relationship to a transcendent, does not mean that contemporary artists or poets or novelists or film-makers admit the reality of God. But it does seem that they are almost obsessed with "the absence of God." They search in anguish for a resolution to their questions and problems, either by discovering that, after all, God is, or by discovering that man can make sense even if there is no divine.

Realizing how profoundly, even "prophetically," the artistic creativity of a people reveals deeper currents of thought and feeling, one wonders if our modern world is really as godless as it sometimes appears. Perhaps ours will prove to be one of the more religious epochs in human history, the time when men discovered that they could turn all their powers of critical analysis to the question of the divine and emerge with a purified and deepened understanding of a God who is real.

Whatever may be the ultimate outcome of contemporary secularity, it is perfectly clear that the question of God is critically important for today's Christians and for all men of faith. There is obviously, no sense at all in religious faith or practice, if God is only the projection of men's own desires and illusions. It serves no purpose whatsoever to talk about revelation, about the word of God to men and men's response to that word, if there is no God. For a community of faith, and for the believers who comprise it, the reality and identity of God is the ultimate question. Unless there is a God, and specifically a God who has revealed himself in Jesus Christ, Christianity has no future, nor should it in justice have one.

Christianity does claim that there is a God, and from the very beginning of its history has claimed that this God can be known with greater or lesser adequacy by men in many different contexts of life. Paul, for example, in his letter to the Romans, distinguishes three stages of man's growth in understanding of God: before the Old Testament revelation, during the Old Testament, and in Christ. The question we will have to study is the validity of each of these ways of knowing the divine, and the manner in which they interact in the Christian's life of faith.

Myths and the Divine

Man seems to have a common-sense, almost instinctive, tendency to explain himself and his world in terms of some "god," no matter how difficult it may be to explain or justify this tendency. As far as we can trace the historical origins of man, there have always been myths by which social groups have attempted to give some intelligibility to their existence and experience. As we saw earlier men tried to explain the power and order that surrounded them in nature and in human society. Lacking the tools and language of formal philosophical analysis, they expressed their insights in the poetic language of myth.

At first glance, many of these myths seem extremely naive. Yet, upon closer examination, they are seen to embody profound insights. However, one wonders if they contained any genuine insight into the reality of the divine, or whether they were simply a projection of human imagination that served the necessary purpose of unifying and directing a social group. Did the myths say anything true about God?

The answer is both "yes" and "no." "Yes," because in their own way the myths reflected an unsophisticated but genuine insight into the principle of causality and its application to the world in which men lived. If things happen, someone or something must have made them happen. Since there are storms, floods, growth of crops, there must be some divinity (or divinities) that causes them. In pointing to some source or cause of the things that happened to them in their lifetime, the ancient peoples who expressed themselves in religious myth were in possession of an element of truth about the divine, namely, that it *is*.

"No" is probably the answer we would have to give, if we asked whether the ancient religious myths said anything true about the *way* in which the transcendent is. It is true that the myths reveal an almost universal awe or fear of the divine, "the holy" which is other than the profane world in which men live out their earthly existence. To this extent, that the myths embody the awareness that the transcendent is not as man is, the mythic insight is legitimate.

It is not the same when the myths attribute to the divine the ways of existing, thinking, deciding, acting that man knows from his own experience. Inevitably, men anthropomorphize the gods they worship, giving to the gods the characteristics of human persons, Men make "god" to their own image and likeness. The divinities lead a fuller and more "elevated" life, but essentially it is the same kind of life that man himself knows. In more intense fashion, the gods have the virtues and foibles of humans.

Thus, while the myths do contain a radical insight into the reality of the transcendent, the anthropomorphic descriptions

of this transcendent led to polytheistic idolatry. Perhaps some
of the better educated and sophisticated persons in these ancient cultures recognized the symbolic character of these
myths and saw beyond the rather crass details of the stories
about the gods. But it seems that the vast bulk of the people
took the myths quite literally, with the result that their religious awareness often degenerated into superstitious fear and
perverted human values.

We know from the Old Testament writings that ancient Israel was threatened by such mythic misunderstandings of the
divine. Surrounded by a culture in which anthropomorphic
description of the gods, strongly sexual in tone, dominated
the religious understandings of the people and found translation in such practices as ritual prostitution, the Israelites
tended to drift away from the view of God that came to them
in revelation. More than once, the teachers in Israel had to
warn the people of the danger of false understandings of the
divine, forbid the making of "graven images," and indicate
the falsity of the gods that their neighbors worshipped.

Despite this strong polemic against the "gods of the Gentiles," the religious faith of Israel absorbed into itself the
deeper level of insight which the myths contained. To a large
extent, the Israelites accepted the poetically expressed cos-
mology of neighboring cultures, even drew from the religious
ritual of other peoples. They differed in regard to the God
whom they believed to be the source of the power and order
and life which the ancient myths were trying to explain.

Israel's faith in Yahweh actually acted as a powerful demythologizing force; we will have to examine this effect more
carefully later. But even within the ancient cultures that developed the myths about the divine there emerged an important critic of religious myth: formal philosophical analysis.

Philosophy and the Divine

Comparative study of religions reveals a recurrent pattern in
the development of man's understanding of life and God. At
the beginning of a culture's history, there is a period in which

the entire people utilize myths unquestioningly as a medium of understanding and explaining human life and experience. There soon arises a more analytic way of examining the realities of man's life in the world, at least among some of the more highly educated. Formal philosophical thought begins to exist side-by-side with the poetic world-view of the myths and, after a time, begins to challenge the accuracy and the adequacy of mythic explanation.

Such philosophical thought can be, and often has been, a purifying influence in a people's culture. Particularly when it is joined to the beginnings of what we would consider "scientific observation" of the world and human society — as happened, for example, in Greece — philosophical reasoning can indicate the falsity of religious myths that too literally attribute human characteristics to the divine. Philosophy need not destroy the religious myths entirely, though at times it has tended to do this. What it can do is to study the symbolic function of myth and to define the limits within which the myth can give acceptable insights. Ultimately, the deepest insights of myth and philosophy coincide, for authentic myth is rooted in basically philosophical insights which are expressed poetically and imaginatively, rather than analytically.

History indicates, however, that the philosophical path to the understanding of the man and God is not without its own problems and dangers. For reasons that are too complex to detail here, most systematic developments of philosophy have tended to lead into a pantheistic view of reality. Whether the philosophical system involved comes to the conclusion that the world is "god" or to the conclusion that the world is illusion and only the divine really exists, the final result is much the same: There is no real distinction between creator and creation, between God and the world.

What seems to be an underlying problem for all such pantheistic philosophies is the difficulty, if not the impossibility, of keeping the divine distinct from the world, if one approaches the divine as being "ultimate perfection." In this approach, the "ultimate" or "the divine" — or whatever name one wants to ascribe to it — is thought to be transcendent in the sense that it is much *more* of what the world is. What the world is in limited fashion, the divine is preeminently — but it is preeminently the same. The intrinsic logic of such a system of thought seems sooner or later to lead to a blurring of distinction between the world and the divine.

Even if philosophy and myth can come to some justifiable knowledge about the divine, this is still a most restricted kind of knowing. Actually there is no direct knowing of God in either approach. What is seen is the intrinsically dependent existence of the world in which men find themselves and of which they are a part. What is directly known is creation, but it is seen to be just that and as therefore indicating the existence of a creator. The divine is not known directly; it is known about.

To say that philosophy cannot lead us to a knowledge of God, but only a knowledge about God, is not in any way to deny the major contribution that philosophy can make to religious thought. Even with the foundation and guidance provided by revelation and tradition, the Christian believer can still impose on God a great deal of anthropomorphic misunderstanding. Christian faith is constantly in need of purification, and the careful distinctions of philosophy are of great value in preventing naively simple notions about God.

When we turn to the faith of Israel and of Christianity as these are expressed in the pages of the Bible, we are confronted with a way of knowing God that is quite different from what we have been examining so far. Whether or not one is a believer and espouses the faith of Israel or of early Christianity, it is evident from the texts of the Bible that those who produced this sacred literature believed that they had a certain direct knowledge of the divine. They not only knew about God, in some mysterious fashion they actually knew him.

This means, then, that one is dealing with a knowledge of God that is qualitatively beyond that which attained in myth or philosophical insight. The knowledge of God that is described in the pages of Scripture springs, not from a grasp of the dependence of the world upon some transcendent cause, but from God's own self-revelation to men. In some way, the divine intervenes specially in human history, making itself known to men in more direct fashion.

The Faith of Israel

Exactly what is involved in the process of revelation, as we see it in the faith-experience of Old Testament Israel, is difficult to ascertain. But apparently, as we saw earlier, it focuses on that situation, most clearly attested to in the case of the great prophetic figures of Old Testament history, in which God makes himself present to the consciousness of men. The experience of the prophet is not that of insight into the fact that there must be a transcendent, or even that of acute awareness of the fact that God is, but rather that of immediate awareness of a God who is communicating personally with him.

Even when one attributes to the prophet's own imagination and memory the sensible elements of the experience that one finds described in Jeremiah 1 or Ezekiel 1, there still remains the hard core of the experience which is most difficult to explain away as psychological projection. The prophet is thoroughly convinced that Yahweh has laid hold of him, and even though he is reluctant to undertake the prophetic role, as Jeremiah was, he cannot escape the word of Yahweh that is given to him to transmit to the people.

If the prophetic experience was actually what the prophets believed it to be, we are dealing with something far beyond the insights of myth and philosophy. Obscure and mysterious though the knowledge might be, the prophet's consciousness somehow contacts the reality of the divine immediately. The prophet knows Yahweh, and so overpowering and new is this knowledge that it forces a "new look" at reality on the part of the prophet and of the people to whom he then proclaims Yahweh's word.

But what understanding of the divine does such a prophetic experience provide? First of all, it makes clear the existence of this God who speaks in revelation. The grounds for realizing the existence of this God are not philosophical reasoning, but immediate and undeniable personal experience. The prophet cannot prove, or even adequately describe, the reality of his experience; he can only bear witness to it, which many prophets did at great personal expense.

Secondly, the God whom the prophet knows is clearly transcendent. Again, the avenue by which his transcendence is understood is quite different from that pursued by rational analysis. The prophet is almost painfully aware that Yahweh is other than he, in the sense that Yahweh is vastly superior and awesome. But he is also aware that Yahweh is "other," because the very situation is one of personal dialogue and relationship, and this could not be possible if the two parties to the dialogue were not radically distinct as persons.

Israel never developed a philosophical movement as such, but involved in her approach to understanding the transcendence of God are some of the most critical philosophical insights attained by man. The personal otherness of the transcendent God seems more surely safeguarded by her confrontation with Yahweh in faith, than by any system of philosophy. Israel did, in the course of her historical development, absorb into her understanding of Yahweh many elements of insight from surrounding religious myths and from the impact of other people's philosophical reflection. But the understanding of Yahweh into which she absorbed them was controlled by the prophetic experience.

Thirdly, this divinity who makes himself known to Israel in the immediacy of familiar relationship is a God who acts on Israel's behalf. Even the key religious experience of Israel's prophets takes place in conjunction with critical happenings in the people's life. These "saving events," beginning with the exodus and the possession of the land, and extending through the centuries of Israel's existence, express Yahweh's attitude towards his people. They are a word by which Yahweh makes clear the kind of divinity he is. Thus Israel learns *about* her God, but this is the same God she knows personally.

The actions of Yahweh indicate that he is a *saving* God. It was his saving activity that freed the people from Egyptian bondage, preserved them from the threats to life that they faced in the desert wanderings, protected them from their more powerful neighbors, and eventually brought them into possession of their own land. He was the all-powerful divinity who overcame the very power of chaos and held it in check, lest it destroy mankind. He was the God who had triumphed even over Israel's own sinfulness and stubbornness, saving the people from themselves.

The notion of the law as a directive from Yahweh reflects the understanding that Yahweh is a God who consciously and deliberately orders things, especially Israel, to some goal. In some way, then, Yahweh thinks and plans and decides. While Israel's notion of *how* Yahweh thinks and plans is strongly anthropomorphic and expressed in imaginative language, the belief that he must do something like our human thinking is rooted in Israel's faith that Yahweh acted in purposeful fashion in her history.

Israel's understanding of her God is largely, then, that he is the God who does these things. Obviously, he is the kind of God who would do such things — an intelligent God, a concerned God, a merciful and forgiving God, a faithful and trustworthy God. In such attributes, the Old Testament literature reflects the faith of Israel about the "inner life" of the God she worshipped. The Israelites believed this God knew all their movements of body and spirit, "their lying down and their rising up." They believed also that to some extent they knew how their god Yahweh thought and acted.

Since the Israelites were an imaginative and poetic people, their view of the "character" of their god was cast in images and metaphor. Yahweh is like a father to Israel; Israel is his son (Hos. 11:1). Yahweh cares for his people as a shepherd cares for his sheep. Particularly when his flock is dispersed in exile because of the infidelity of Israel's leadership, it is Yah-

168   CHRISTIAN COMMUNITY: RESPONSE TO REALITY

weh himself who will gather together the scattered sheep from
every hillside and lead them once more to safe and abundant
pasturage (Ezek. 34). Most frequently, Yahweh is described
in the figure of a husband: He is the faithful spouse who
raises up Israel from her insignificance, makes her his bride,
remains faithful despite her adulterous flirtations with false
gods, and wins back her affection.

In all such poetic passages we are dealing with metaphor.
The Old Testament thinkers are not saying that Yahweh is
literally the father, or the shepherd, or the spouse of the people, but are attempting to express what the relation of Yahweh to his people is by comparing Yahweh to father, shepherd, husband. Still, the attribution of these terms was not totally arbitrary; there was something in Israel's faith-insight
about God that served as the basis for applying such deeply
personal images to him. When the prophets, with their unique
religious experience of God, tried to convey to their contemporaries the kind of God they had encountered, these particular metaphorical images "fit" better than anything else they
could draw from human experience.

In the last analysis, what insight into the being of the divine can the faith of Israel give us, even if we accept as val-
idly rooted in "revelation" the understandings her people
had? Even if their faith was the result of God's special self-
revelation, what can it tell us about the "personal" life of
God himself, since by Israel's own mature admission this god
Yahweh is far beyond the thoughts of man (Is. 55)? All we
can ultimately answer to such questions must be in terms of
Israel's faith as we know it from the Old Testament texts.
That faith reflects for us the God of the Old Testament as he
revealed himself, for it was in that faith that the revelation
took place.

But if the revelation did take place in Israel's faith awareness of Yahweh, it took place in inseparable conjunction with
the other elements of Israel's life-experience. There were not
two "worlds of experience" that made up the consciousness
of the Old Testament people. There was one experience in

which their faith in Yahweh's reality and activity conditioned their understanding of everything that happened to them.

We must not suppose, however, that all the Israelites lived at a high pitch of religious awareness, constantly conscious of the presence of Yahweh. The condemnations of the prophets make it perfectly clear that the bulk of the people found it only too easy to drift into a forgetfulness of Yahweh; it was the prophetic task to awaken the people to the deeper dimensions of the reality that they were encountering in their daily life. What is significant for us as we attempt to discover the "message" of Old Testament revelation is the fact that the prophets did not, in their attempt to convert their contemporaries to a knowledge of Yahweh, direct men's minds away from the events of ordinary life. Instead, they tried to lead their hearers to a faith-insight into those events.

Perhaps the most basic "fact" about the divine to be drawn from Old Testament faith is that God wishes to be known by men, for he reveals himself to them. This implies that he wishes — for reasons that are profoundly obscure — to exist in some kind of personal relationship with men. Why else would he thus communicate with them?

This conclusion raises serious problems. When one ponders philosophically the question of God's existence and being, it seems almost incredible that there could ever be this kind of communion between the divine and the human. But this is the faith of Israel: Their God did make himself present and active in their history; he did speak to them over many centuries, through Moses and the prophets; he did expect of them to enter into dialogue with him through the response of faith and worship. If this faith of Israel is objectively justified, then we are dealing with a way of knowing God that is uniquely different from that involved in philosophical or mythic understanding of the transcendent.

Jesus and the Divine

With Jesus of Nazareth, as Christian faith views him — God's own Word incarnated — a second "qualitative leap" occurs in the process of man's knowledge of the divine. The letter to the Hebrews points to this leap in its opening verses:

> In many and various ways God spoke of old to our fathers by the prophets; but in these last days he has spoken to us by a Son, whom he appointed the heir of all things, through whom also he created the world. He reflects the glory of God and bears the very stamp of his nature, upholding the universe by his word of power (Heb. 1:1-3).

Jesus continues and fulfills the prophetic revelation of Old Testament Israel, but goes far beyond it.

As we approach a study of the unique function of Jesus in the process of revelation, it is essential not to deprive him of his authentic humanity. Christians have, at times, been inclined to exalt Christ to the point of obscuring his humanness. In fidelity to official Church teaching, such as the classical formulation of the Council of Chalcedon in 451 which insisted on Christ's possession of both divine and human nature, these Christians have repeated the teaching that Jesus had a true human nature. But they tended to deny to Jesus a genuine human life-experience, an experience that involved learning and uncertain expectation of the future, anxiety and planning and true use of freedom in decision. Instead, they attributed to Jesus in his earthly life a most unearthly kind of knowledge: infused ideas about all things, so that no learning was even possible, much less needed, and some kind of "preliminary beatific vision," which deprived his ordinary life-experience of any purpose other than to make him appear human.

If one takes seriously the Christian belief that Jesus of Nazareth was (and is) the incarnate Son of God, the human consciousness of Jesus is without parallel in human experience. There are dimensions to it that surpass incomparably the deepest reaches of understanding attained by other men. There are also levels of his human understanding that are like our own, levels that can and actually did find expression in regular human language and actions. So thoroughly human was Jesus that his contemporaries, prior to his public ministry, never suspected that he was other than just another man — "Is not this the carpenter's son?"

During Jesus' earthly life, those who dealt with him came into immediate contact with his human consciousness in the same manner in which any of us deal with one another in ordinary conversation. For Christians today who would try to reach an awareness of Jesus there are manifold problems. One could, of course, lapse into an uncritical attitude, assuming that the way he already thinks about Christ, both in his earthly life and in his risen state, is quite accurate and sufficient. To do this would be to overlook the depths of the mystery that Christ is; it would be to abandon the search to discover the true reality of the divine as it is manifested in Christ.

At first glance the New Testament texts seem to give us a direct and detailed report of the mentality of Jesus during the years of his public ministry. His activity is described at length, and his teaching preserved in the pages of the Gospels. Modern Scripture scholarship has taught us, though, that we cannot approach the New Testament writings with this oversimplified view. The Gospel accounts are not meant to be biography, although they are dealing with the events of Jesus' life and death and resurrection. The writings of the New Testament are expressions of the faith of the early Church, the record of its belief in the unique meaning of Jesus and of what he had done. They tell us, not just what Jesus said and did, but the deeper significance of those words and deeds. The Jesus of the Gospels is the Jesus of history, but the Jesus of history as remembered by a community that believed in him as the Lord.

The purpose of the New Testament writings was in large part catechetical. The oral traditions out of which the New Testament books grew, and the writings themselves, were intended to acquaint Christians with an understanding of their own lives which derived from the event of Jesus' death and resurrection. Selection of scenes from Jesus' public ministry and of sayings from his teaching was governed by this catechetical purpose, as was the precise way in which the scenes were described and the sayings formulated. This does not mean that we have no contact through the Gospels with what Jesus actually said or did, but it does mean that we may not naively assume that the Gospels record direct citations from Jesus' words.

The Christians who produced the New Testament literature were already living under the full impact of Christ's resurrection. While they were perfectly aware that this Lord in whom they believed had lived in sensible form, had taught and ministered to people, they could not divorce themselves from the realization of his identity and role as they knew these through his resurrection. Inevitably, as they recalled Jesus' earthly life and activity during those years, they saw this as leading up to and preparing for the essential saving action of his death and resurrection.

In trying to study the reality of Jesus' human consciousness during the years of his public ministry, we must proceed cautiously and humbly, not reading into it our own religious or theological presuppositions. At the same time, we need not conclude, as some contemporary scholars have done, that there is no possibility of knowing anything about the historical Jesus and therefore no purpose in undertaking such a search. The very existence of the Gospels as we have them indicates that the early Christians wanted people to know about the earthly ministry of Christ. For that reason, these Christians would have given an account of the ministry which was substantially drawn from what actually happened to Jesus in the years immediately before his death and resurrection.

Also, if one recalls the dominant theological view of Jesus in the Gospels — namely, that he is the fulfillment of Israel's historical role — this would seem to indicate that the early Christians have a special interest in what Jesus actually did and said during his public ministry. As Israel's Messiah, Jesus' own life-experience had an intrinsic function in realizing the potential of Old Testament history as revelation.

We are justified, then, in drawing to some extent from the New Testament writings in our attempt to study the human awareness of Jesus, particularly his human awareness of the divine. Yet, to avoid inaccuracy as far as possible, it might be well to restrict ourselves to the most fundamental aspects of Jesus' activity and teaching, to those elements of the Gospel account that underlie any of the details or any of the exact wordings of his teaching. Even within such limitations, we can draw some extremely significant conclusions.

What seems incontestable, if the Gospel accounts are not totally misleading with regard to Jesus' life, is the fact that he lived his human experience with a constant awareness of his Father. There can be little doubt that Jesus actually did carry on a ministry of prophetic teaching; to deny this would be to deny the entire context of the Gospel accounts. It also seems undeniable that the one theme running through all the teaching of Jesus was his Father. He was at pains to clarify for his auditors the true nature of the Father, to disabuse them of their inadequate or faulty understandings of the divine, to convey to them some of his own insight into the "personality" of the Father.

If this is true — and we will have to examine it further in just a moment — we are in contact with a fact of inestimable importance in our search for the reality of the divine. It would mean that this man, Jesus, stood in a unique relationship to the divine, one in which he was conscious of himself having the relation of son to God. Jesus would, naturally, have had those understandings of the divine that we might refer to as "philosophical insights," even though he would have had no opportunity to obtain formalized philosophical understanding. He would have seen the order and power in the universe as being the result of divine power and governance. He also possessed those understandings of the divine that would have been the religious heritage of any Jew of his day, for he grew up with and was formed by the Scriptures and liturgy of Judaism. But beyond these two ways of knowing the divine, there was the way that was unique to him: the personal knowing of God as his own Father. This manner of knowing would have absorbed into itself the other two levels of human awareness of God.

This certainly is the way in which the New Testament literature speaks about Jesus' human awareness of his Father. If nothing more, this view tells us that early Christianity believed that Jesus lived in and experienced a most exceptional relationship to God. The early Christians saw that Jesus was God's own Son, not in a metaphorical sense, but actually. With his resurrection, Jesus entered into the full awareness of his transcendent relationship, but even during the years before his death his human awareness was already dominated by the reality of his Father.

As early Christians viewed him, Jesus of Nazareth was a man specially sent from God. His mission stood in continuity with the role of the Old Testament prophets and of Moses himself, but it was intrinsically superior to theirs. Many of the New Testament texts indicate this, but we might take as an example the parable of the unjust custodians of the vineyard, a parable common to all three synoptic Gospels.

The parable is one of the most interesting in the Gospels, for it is not just a story told to illustrate a point, but is, in short and parable form, a summary of the Old Testament prophetic movement. Its basic imagery is the familiar Old Testament prophetic figure of Israel as the vineyard planted by Yahweh (cf. Is. 5). In the Gospels (Mt. 21:33), the parable begins by telling how the owner of the vineyard had planted and cared for it; then, when he went into a far country, he left the vineyard with caretakers. Each year at the time of vintage he sent messengers to obtain the revenue from the vineyard. The caretakers, however, did not pay the revenue; instead they attacked the messengers violently, even killing some of them. As a final measure, the owner of the vineyard decided to send his own son, but he, too, was slain by the ruthless caretakers.

The parable is obviously directed at the Jewish leadership and refers to the death of Jesus at their hands. What is of special interest to our present discussion is the contrast made in the parable between the servants who were sent earlier to collect the revenue and the son whom the owner finally sends. Here we find Jesus both related to and contrasted with the prophets of Israel. He comes to undertake the same task that had been theirs, but he is not just another of them — he is the son.

Texts such as this show that the early Christians looked on Jesus as being God's own son in a unique fashion. Exactly how they came to this realization is not completely clear, but the Gospel texts seem to indicate that at least part of the insight was rooted in Jesus' own references to his Father in his public teaching. His teaching was constantly concerned with his Father, and he seems to have viewed his own public activity as the work of establishing his Father's kingdom. The Gospels tell us that Jesus was totally dedicated to fulfilling his Father's will, to carrying out the task his Father had given him to do.

Again, it seems from the Gospel texts — even when one allows for the extent to which they are theological reflection on the fact of Jesus' death and resurrection — that a major factor in Jesus' own human self-identification was his relationship to God as his Father. It is next to impossible for us to recover the human self-awareness of Jesus — what it meant for him to exist in this special relationship to God. What is recoverable is the fact that there was this relationship of familiarity and immediacy. Jesus gave expression to this consciousness that was his by referring to God as his Father.

While the use of this term "father" by Jesus was first and foremost a means of naming this God to whom he felt himself specially related, it also opened the way to attributing to God the characteristics associated with human fatherhood. The heavenly Father, as the Gospels portray him for us, is all that the ideal father should be. He is personally and deeply concerned about others; he is understanding and merciful; he is faithful and dependable.

When we recall that it is the transcendent God to whom

the Gospels are referring, it seems almost contradictory to speak of him as "personally concerned" about human beings. There appears to be an opposition between the immutability and impassibility of a creator (as philosophical insight would understand him) and the kind of personal involvement connected with a notion like "being concerned for men." The Gospel teaching, however, is unmistakable; the parable of the prodigal son is a classic illustration of it.

It is impossible to read this parable (Mt. 15:11), and think of Jesus' Father as living in abstract detachment from human needs. The father of the prodigal is obviously worried about the welfare of his wayward son, longs for his return, and is overjoyed at the prodigal's return. Obviously, we can not attribute such "states of consciousness" to God with complete literalness, but the parable is meaningless if it does not give us some insight into the relation of God to men.

Again, one can gain some insight into the Father's "attitude of mercy" towards men, not just from what is contained in Jesus' teaching, but from Jesus' own activity. The Gospel describes Jesus as acting on the basis of what he thought his Father wished him to do. In being not only tolerant and forgiving of human shortcomings, but actually tender and solicitous towards those who were considered "sinners," Jesus was obviously acting as he thought his Father wished him to act. In this way, he gave expression more graphically than he could have done by words to his understanding of the Father's mercy towards men.

As a devout Jew, Jesus would have thought of his Father as "a faithful God," since fidelity to his promises is one of the attributes most constantly associated with Yahweh by Old Testament thought. Yet, in the career of Jesus, especially in the mounting opposition he encountered and in its culmination in his apprehension and death, we see that his perception of God's fidelity was of a more profound and personal nature. Because his Father was that — a father — he would not allow Jesus to be ultimately overcome by his enemies, even by death. It was to this fidelity that Christ bore witness by decisively encountering death.

The early Christians did not miss the point of this witness. For them the Father of our Lord, Jesus Christ, had definitively proved his fidelity to his promises by raising up Jesus from the dead (Acts 2:30-32). Not only did he manifest himself as a faithful God, he made it supremely evident that he was a life-giving God. The new life in the risen Christ was the pledge and source of life for all mankind.

The Faith of Christians

Christ's resurrection provided an entirely new context in which the disciples of Jesus could come to a realization of the identity of the Father, as well as of Jesus himself. Since Jesus' teaching had been for them a medium for understanding this Father about whom he spoke and to whom he was specially related, their discovery of Jesus' full identity as it was manifested to them in his resurrection opened up new avenues for understanding the divine. The first Christians' experience of the presence of the risen Christ, their dawning realization that he was truly the Lord, their awareness of the Spirit abiding with them and guiding their community existence, gave them a perspective for understanding God which was far beyond that possessed by even the greatest of Old Testament sages or prophets (Lk. 7:26-28).

To delineate the various elements of this resurrection-faith of the early Church and the insight into the divine that it contains would take, literally, almost forever, for this task would involve a definitive understanding of the entire New Testament text, a goal the Church will be pursuing for the remainder of her historical existence. One element in this understanding, however, seems to be particularly important and also seems to indicate the characteristically new approach to the understanding of the divine that was made possible with the incarnation of the Word in Jesus of Nazareth. This new element is the fact that in the historically existing reality which is Jesus' relationship to the person he calls his Father, God is the pole of that relationship.

The most appropriate way for Christians to think of God is as "the Father of our Lord, Jesus Christ." The denomination of God as Father by Christians is not essentially a matter of attributing to him those qualities that would characterize an ideal father. It is, rather, naming God in terms of an existing relation, one pole of which is the historically ascertainable personage, Jesus of Nazareth. In so doing, Christian faith is speaking, not so much about *what* God is as *who* he is, since persons are constituted as such by their relationships to other persons.

In this perspective, the Christian approach to the understanding of God is both the continuation and the realization of Israel's understanding of the divine. As we saw earlier, Israel's faith is characterized by the manner in which her view of Yahweh is grounded in historical events — "I am the god who brought your fathers out of the land of Egypt." In Christianity, God is known in and through the event of the life and death and resurrection of Jesus. It is in terms of this historical happening, and of its trans-historical continuation in the mystery of Jesus' resurrected life, that present-day Christians can refer to God as "our Father."

When one compares this way of understanding the divine with the way employed by myth or philosophy, one can see how unique the former is. The denomination of God as "the Father of our Lord, Jesus Christ" does not require any extrapolation of human or created attributes; it is a name that is given on the basis of the historical and the existent. The denomination is in terms of the reality which is Jesus. God is the one whose son Jesus is, he is the one of whom this Jesus was aware, he is the one whose will Jesus strove to fulfill, he is the one who raised Jesus from death.

Ultimately, this means that Christianity is essentially non-mythical and should be able to withstand the kind of dissolution that affects mythical religions when they are subjected to philosophical or scientific analysis. We are far enough today into the process of critical thought about religion to see that careful "demythologizing" is a benefit to Christianity, for it purifies faith, removes false interpretations of Christianity, and makes clearer the depth of the mystery that is proper to Christian belief.

Christianity is faith in mystery, that mystery which is Jesus, Christ and Lord, in whom the divine is revealed to men. Jesus is mystery, not because he is hidden but because he is the opposite; as the Word of God made man the purpose of his human existing is to be a revelation. He is mystery because the reality of his existence and experience as man forms an intrinsic continuity with the reality of the divine. He is God's own son become man.

For Christian faith, Jesus of Nazareth is the sacrament of the divine. It is he who reveals and makes present his Father. This is why the New Testament Scriptures can describe him as superior to the prophets, superior to the Jerusalem Temple. Both prophet and Temple had functioned in Old Testament times as a sign of God's presence to his people. Jesus is not only a sign of that presence, he is Emmanuel, God-with-us. Because of his coming, Old Testament prophecy no longer has a purpose for being. Because he is the unique dwelling of God with men, the Temple can no longer serve as a privileged symbol of God's saving presence.

What seems to be involved in this contrast of Jesus to both prophet and Temple is the fact that he now is the supreme "contact point" between men and God. It is in Christ that the Father reveals himself to men; it is in Christ that men attain to union with this Father. To no other human consciousness has the reality of God been so immediately and fully present. To no other man has God been so fully revealed. "For the law was given through Moses; grace and truth came through Jesus Christ. No one has ever seen God; the only Son, who is in the bosom of the Father, he has made him known" (Jn. 1:17-18).

It is not just a matter of this man Jesus having had an insight into the divine which was far beyond that accorded to other men, an insight which he could then transmit to others. As John's Gospel tells us, all that Jesus is and becomes humanly — throughout his life and into his resurrection — is divine word spoken humanly. Jesus is the very Word of the Father enfleshed. Not only what Jesus said and did, but also what he was and is as man, is revelation; it is the translation into humanly graspable form of the mystery of God being for men.

If Christian faith about Jesus is true, if Jesus is the Word of God become man, then Jesus is the resolution of the age-old opposition between the transcendence and the immanence of the divine. Religions had always seemed forced to choose between the two attributes: either their divinity was truly transcendent, distinct from and other than creation, or he was involved in and somehow himself part of creation. The first alternative tended to set the divinity so far apart that men could have no contact with him whatsoever; the second alternative often ended in pantheism. In Christ, both immanence and transcendence are safeguarded. His Father is clearly the infinite creator of the universe, and Jesus himself is the Word who was with the Father from the beginning and through whom the world was created (Jn. 1:1-3). Yet, the Word incarnated, the man Jesus, is an intrinsic part of the historical process of the world's development. More than that, he is from within the historical process the very source and purpose of that development (Eph. 1:1-10).

It is difficult to find a passage in the New Testament writings that states more profoundly this "entry" of God into human life and consciousness than the eleventh chapter of Matthew's Gospel. The entire chapter depicts Jesus as the epitome of wisdom. As the chapter begins, the disciples of John the Baptist approach Jesus with the question: "Are you he who is to come, or shall we look for another?" In response, Jesus tells John's followers to report what they have seen and heard: the blind see, the lame walk. What he says, in effect, is that his deeds are his justification. Somewhat later in the chapter (v. 19), Jesus says, "Yet wisdom is justified by her deeds." The implication is clear: Jesus is wisdom.

Yet men will not accept wisdom when it is offered to them,

for they do not wish to accept the implications. They are like little children who keep changing the rules of a game when they dislike the way in which things are going. John the Baptist had advocated fasting, and they had dismissed him as possessed. Jesus himself came, and ate and drank with men, and he was accused of gluttony and drunkenness. But because they had rejected the wisdom that he brought them, the cities in which he had preached were doomed to extinction.

The source of Jesus' unique wisdom is described in the prayer he addresses to his Father: "All things have been delivered to me by my Father; and no one knows the Son except the Father, and no one knows the Father except the Son and anyone to whom the Son chooses to reveal him." Obviously, there is question here of a special manner of knowing, the kind that the Father has of Christ. Yet Christ as the Son possesses such a knowledge of the Father, because the Father has communicated himself totally to this Son. No other man can lay claim to such knowledge of God, unless Jesus himself shares with him this understanding of the Father.

Two things emerge clearly from this richly theological passage: the unparalleled role of Jesus in the process of revelation, and the fact that others can somehow share in the knowledge of God that he himself possesses. Because he is the Father's own Son, Jesus knows the Father in privileged fashion — the Father has held back nothing in his self-communication to his Son. Only to Jesus is the fullness of divine revelation given, but out of this fullness he gives to his followers some of the same understanding of the Father that he has. His function in the work of revelation is central and irreplaceable: Only he who is the Son can tell us that the very "person" whom men refer to as "God" is *his* Father.

Such New Testament passages seem to promise an unprecedented opportunity for men to understand the reality of the divine. Jesus, who is himself a man and who can therefore convey humanly his own immediate knowledge of the Father, acts as mediator in the process of revelation and shares with believers his own insight into the divine. But the problem is not that easily solved, for there is the question of how this sharing take place. The problem becomes more acute when we reflect that Jesus himself came into his full human understanding of himself and of his Father only with entry into risen life. Having passed into the situation of resurrection-life, where our ordinary human patterns of communication can no longer link us with him, how can he convey to us the consciousness he now has of the Father, of himself as the Son, and of the divine Spirit in whom he and the Father find communion and loving self-expression?

As we saw, Christians can, and should, find some recourse in this difficulty to the historical event of Jesus. As Christian faith accepts him, Jesus knew and knows his Father directly. Believing this, a Christian can understand that God is the Father of Christ. This truth is rich in implications for human life, but if it is no more than a piece of "factual" knowledge, it is not really satisfying. The man of faith wishes to know the Father personally; he cannot but voice the plea of Philip at the Last Supper: "Lord, show us the Father, and we shall be satisfied" (Jn. 14:8).

Jesus' response to Philip's request is of profound importance for any understanding of the process of Christian revelation. His words indicate the sacramentality of Jesus' humanness: whoever sees Jesus is actually seeing the Son, and thus sees the Father also. This is true because this Son is the Father's own Word. Just as we know other human persons through their words, so that person who is the Father is known personally in his Son who is his Word. It is not as if Christ spoke about his Father, and the Father himself was not present to those who heard Christ; because Christ is his own proper Word that he speaks to men, the Father is present to men in and through Christ. Christ is the sacrament of the Father, because by his own intrinsic significance he makes the Father present to the faith and consciousness of men.

We are still left, however, with a large measure of our problem: How do we hear this Word which is the risen

Christ, even if we are believers? For it would seem, in the light of what we have already seen, that Christ can function as sacrament of the Father only if he himself is somehow personally known by men. Only to know *about* him, even if that entailed a religious acceptance of his unique identity and function, would not bring one into contact with his personhood, and apparently it is this latter that is meant to be Word of the Father.

The Role of the Spirit

Part, at least, of the answer is suggested by the New Testament teaching about the Spirit. Having passed through death into the fullness of human life that is resurrection, Christ poured out upon his followers his own Spirit, so that this Spirit might animate and unite them into a community of faith. The Spirit does not replace Christ as the indwelling principle of unification; rather, it is in this Spirit that the risen Christ is rendered present to those who will accept him in faith.

This Spirit, shared in by all men of faith, is Christ's own Spirit, the expression of his own sonship, the source of his own human power to redeem mankind. It is in this Spirit that Christ himself attained to the full human awareness of his unique sonship, and to the full human awareness of his Father. By sharing in this Spirit of Christ, Christians are meant to become conscious of their own participation in Christ's sonship. Knowing themselves as sons, they will know that Father whose sons they are.

John's Gospel (14:26) reflects the experience of early Christianity that the presence of the Spirit leads to a deepened understanding of both Christ and the Father. "The Counselor, the Holy Spirit, whom the Father will send in my name, he will teach you all things, and bring to mind all that I have said to you." Jesus had talked to his disciples about himself and about his Father. The deeper realization of what he had said came with the Pentecostal gift of the Spirit.

If the texts of the New Testament are any indication, the

presence and reality of Christ's Spirit is impossible to define. Joined together into a community of faith in the risen Christ, Christians can experience together the power and impetus and consolation of the Spirit, but the experience defies precise verbal description. Yet the Spirit is truly discernible in the community's awareness of its own Christian faith, of the Christian love that welds it into a community, and of its relationship to the Father. As Paul tells the Galatians (Gal. 4:6), it is in the Spirit that Christians have faith, sonship with Christ, and the ability to address God as "Abba, Father," the same familiar term of personal relationship that Jesus himself used (Mk. 14:36).

To speak this way about the knowledge of Christ and the Father that Christians are meant to have in the Spirit indicates the necessary role of prayer in Christian faith. Abstract understanding about the reality of the divine, even if it is controlled by accurate study of the New Testament texts, does not constitute "knowing God" as the Bible speaks of it. What is required is a conscious acceptance of and response to the loving presence of Christ and the Father — which is exactly what prayer is all about.

But when one is dealing with such a profoundly personal approach to the divine, what assurance is there that a Christian — or a community of Christians — is being guided in its faith and life by the Spirit of Christ, and is not following some erroneous idea? The Church's experience, even in the early decades of her existence, shows that not all who claim to be illumined and moved by the Spirit are justified in that claim. The Church has possessed many true prophets, but the integrity of her faith has also been threatened by many misguided visionaries and self-appointed "teachers of orthodoxy."

In his own earthly ministry, Christ could provide for this necessary clarification of the Spirit's action. His own words and deeds gave expression to the Spirit who worked through him; it was through his works and teaching that he communicated the Spirit to those who believed in him. With his resur-

rection a new normative expression of the Spirit was required. This is the Christian community itself in its corporate
life of faith.

The Church: Sacrament of Christ

Early in its existence — certainly as early as Paul's letters
to the Church at Corinth — the primitive Christian community began to realize that it itself was part of the continuing
mystery of Christ. He, the risen Lord, was so intimately present to and united with those who believed in him that the
Christian community was truly his body. Obviously, the use
of the term "body" to describe the Church's relationship to
Christ is a figure of speech, but it is more than that. In a real
sense, the Christian community is meant to do for Christ
much of what a body does for a human person: it is the principle of locating the risen Christ's presence and activity in the
context of space and time; it is the externalization that is
meant to give expression to the conscious human intent of
Christ; it is the "instrument" through which the risen Lord
continues to carry out his salvific work in the lives of men.

Thus, the Church is meant to be a sacrament of Christ,
somewhat the way Jesus was sacrament of the Father. Not
only does the Christian community by its existence among
men testify to the fact that Christ, though risen, is still present
to us; it itself, as a community of faith, makes Christ present
to the world. Through the Church, his body, Christ "extends"
his work of revealing the Father throughout the remainder of
human history. Because of this, the role of the Church is basically prophetic. The Church truly speaks for Christ and gives
utterance to his Spirit, which is the Spirit of prophecy.

This means that everything about the Christian community
is meant to be "word of God" to men. In her total life, but
more explicitly in her proclamation of Scripture and in her
celebration of sacrament, the Church is meant to speak to
men of faith the revelation of the Father in his Son and his
Spirit. Thus the Church guides the faith of her own members
and indicates the true action of the Spirit.

If one accepts this faith-insight into the nature and function of the Christian community, he possesses a most important guideline for knowing God authentically. A Christian today who wishes to know Christ personally, and through him the Father, is not meant to build for himself some imaginative picture of the risen Christ, nor is he to pretend that he is back at the scenes described in the Gospels and relating to Jesus in that context. Instead, he should direct his attention and perception to the living Church of today, to that community of people that sacramentalizes the presence of Christ now. In viewing his own Christian brethren with the eyes of faith, the Christian is actually in direct contact with the mystery of the risen Christ.

Ultimately, this is the deepest meaning and purpose of the Christian Church in history. This Church is not just a group of people who follow the teachings of Jesus, or a group that adheres to religious institutions claiming their origin in Jesus. Rather, the risen Christ abides with those men and women who accept him in faith; their faith-acceptance makes it possible for him to communicate himself in deepening presence to their consciousness and their love. To be a Christian is to bear in one's life and one's person the mystery of the risen Christ.

Obviously, we are dealing with something that is in the realm of faith, and with faith as it confronts the unfathomable mystery of the Word of God become man. Within that context of faith the kind of knowledge of Christ and his Father that we have been describing can be authentic and maturely-balanced human experience. Through exposure to the faith of his fellow-Christians, and through the gradual growth of his own experience of Christian life, a man is meant to develop an increasing awareness of the reality of Christ, of the Spirit he shares with his fellow Christians, of the Father who reveals himself in Christ and the Spirit.

Knowledge of God, then, is meant to come within the experience of human life itself. Sharing the experience of faith and life with the other members of the Christian community, which itself is meant at any given moment in history to be immersed in the experience of mankind, a Christian should discover in this very experience the saving presence of God. While this is an experience in faith, and therefore an experience of mystery, the Christian is not dealing with a mystery that is hidden from him by the sensible realities of his ordinary human life, but one that is revealed within that life.

For Christian faith, God is properly and personally known as the Father who reveals himself in his Word and his Spirit. This far transcends the clearest and most profound insights of philosophy, and goes well beyond even the faith of Old Testament Israel. Nevertheless, it denies none of the truth that these two "ways" to God contain; instead, it sees that all this truth applies to that Father whom Christ reveals. Christian insistence on the position of the Father as "the ultimate reality" does nothing to diminish appreciation for the reality of the created world, for it is in that world that the presence of God is to be discovered; it is that world which sacramentalizes the God who reveals himself to men.

In some ways, it could be said that the Christian is the man who most treasures "the secular." Or perhaps it would be better to say that the Christian cannot, in the last analysis, admit a dichotomy between the sacred and the secular. For him, the whole of created reality, especially his experience of life within the Christian community, is meant to be the sacrament of the presence of Christ, who himself is the sacrament of the Father. All creation shares in the revelation of God, though in varying degrees, and the very action of God in creating the world is seen to coincide with his action of revealing himself in his Son.

When all is said and done, however, the Christian's answer to the question, "Who is God?" is very simple: God is the Father of our Lord, Jesus Christ. He is our Father who reveals us to himself in his Son and his Spirit.